Chez Marc's
Quarantine Cookbook

Marc S. Pollack

MARRO PUBLISHING
Atlanta, Georgia

This book is dedicated to my food critic and partner of 47 years, Robin Pollack. Over the course of her career as Critic, she also made all the plates and bowls used in this book.

TABLE OF CONTENTS

INTRODUCTION: Remember that Day? — 8

A WELL-STOCKED KITCHEN — 11

EQUIPMENT —12

FRESH PRODUCE —13

A DAY WITHOUT WINE IS A DAY WITHOUT SUNSHINE —14

APPETIZERS —16

SALADS & SOUP—32

FISH—50

MEAT—72

EGGS, SANDWICHES, & STARCHES—96

VEGETABLES & SIDES—124

DRINKS—136

INDEX—141

ACKNOWLEDGMENTS—144

Remember that day?

When my wife, Robin, and I went into COVID-19 quarantine with much of the rest of the country on Friday, March 13, 2020, I immediately turned to a favorite pastime, cooking, in order to keep busy and stay healthy and positive about the experience. What we thought would be a short "shelter-in-place" act of survival, became a journey of self-discovery, as well as a greater appreciation of home cooking. I worked constantly under the critical eye of Robin, and we feasted daily on the bounty available from Robin's garden, as well as farm-fresh foods available locally, items from wholesalers and specialty grocers, via online shopping and home deliveries.

For the next sixty-seven days, from mid-March through mid-May, I cooked three meals every day without repeating any menus. I was inspired by the best ingredients available in our garden and at our local grocery stores, and I became adept at early morning shopping without any crowds, wearing a mask and social distancing. Although I didn't repeat any specific recipe, I did create many variations with similar ingredients in different preparations, and in different combinations of side dishes. Some of our most interesting and creative dishes surfaced by using leftovers from a prior dinner to make subsequent lunches. There were no limits to our creativity, other than trying to keep it simple. Our personal journey is organized to offer you some interesting combinations, with drink and wine pairings. We've organized this book to provide some insights into how we combined menus with sides and vegetable dishes in new and interesting ways. Feel free to experiment—there are no rules at Chez Marc.

Quarantine, it turns out, wasn't all that bad; in fact, it kept us safe and healthy in more ways than one. We created wonderful diversions with food, wine, and self-indulgence, as well as finding enjoyment through virtual yoga and pilates, swimming, walking, Peloton cycling, gardening, organizing our space, and of course, Zooming—the new normal.

The food and drink recipes that are included in this cookbook are simple to make and simply delicious. We are true believers in the notion that the quality of cooking is directly related to the quality of the ingredients used, so I advise you not to skimp on either quality or freshness. Additionally, I was a bit surprised that my essential equipment (tongs, spatulas, spoons, knives, etc.) became my best friends and helpers. You can't minimize the importance of a well-stocked pantry and a well-equipped kitchen.

I do recommend a few basic steps to daily cooking. I strongly suggest that you define your cooking area and clear it of all clutter before you begin. Then, I suggest you organize yourself with all necessary tools, equipment, and ingredients to create a *mis-en-place*, a French culinary term that simply means "everything in place." Read through your recipe, get out the necessary tools, and measure your ingredients out carefully into small plates or bowls. Don't rush. Now you're ready to cook.

Another thing I find important in most everything I cook is the combination of basic ingredients used in many dishes from various cultures—usually a combination of diced vegetables sautéed 'til translucent. In classic French cuisine there is the concept of *mirepoix* (meer-PWAH), a flavor base made up of onions, celery, and carrots, generally in a ratio of 2:1:1. In Italian cooking, mirepoix is known as *soffrito*, and it often includes chopped tomatoes. In Cajun/Creole cuisine, for which I have a great affinity, a similar flavor base is called the "holy trinity" and includes onions, celery, and bell peppers, generally in a ratio of 2:1:1. Of course, alternatives to these base flavors can always be added, including things like garlic and tomatoes. As a guide, when cooking a dish that serves four, start with 1 cup of diced onions and ½ cup of the other two ingredients. It's always fascinated me that many cultures have similar dishes that go by different names, based on differing local ingredients.

We celebrated our first socially distanced meal on May 2, 2020, after fifty-one days of quarantine. It was good to interact with other humans, particularly friends, in person, even if we were outside and six feet apart. I suspect this is a small taste of the new normal.

I show several recipes in combination with other dishes to illustrate menu possibilities. I'm big on plating and combining colors and textures to make a dish look good. Visual sense is as important as smell and taste in making a wonderful dish. Hopefully you will take this away from all of the photos included in this book.

Here's a bit about Chez Marc: I've been cooking since I left home at age eighteen. I took it up in college, since no one else would cook anything I really liked. I've had very little formal training, with the exception of a couple of classes at cooking supply shops, some TV shows (I've learned much from Julia Child and Jacques Pépin on PBS shows), and a couple of weeks at cooking school, Culinary Boot Camp at the CIA. I have a very utilitarian approach to cooking. That is, I like to cook because I like to eat, and I cook for others because I like to make people happy. I'm a hedonist at heart.

I hope by the time you read this, we are free to safely share a table again. For this time, however, and beyond, I offer these recipes and dishes, along with photos, for your family enjoyment.

A Well-Stocked Kitchen

The quality of cooking *is* directly related to the products used. Don't skimp on product quality.

I keep these essential foods on hand all the time: onions, garlic, carrots, celery, and all colors of sweet peppers.

Additionally, it's necessary to have various oils to cook with—some that can stand high temperatures (grapeseed, canola, peanut), and some oils for finishing (high quality extra-virgin olive oil).

Basic cooking equipment is essential, and all equipment should be easily accessible. I love my tongs, spatulas, and spoons. A great pair of scissors and/or poultry shears are important to have. There's no substitute for sturdy, well balanced, and sharp knives, including at a minimum: a paring knife, a butcher's knife, a serrated knife, and a tomato knife. I started with German steel and have gravitated over the years to Japanese knives. A sharpening stone is essential, along with a honing stick. Don't, under any circumstances, use electric knife sharpeners; go to your local kitchen store for sharpening if you don't have a stone.

Here's a short list of useful things to have:

Slicing and butcher's knife,
   6 to 8-inches
A good cutting board
Knife sharpening stone
Tongs (my favorite)
Kitchen scissors
Small tasting spoons
Grater
Rubber silicon spatula
Cheese knife/slicer
Serving spoons
Stainless steel fish spatula

Equipment

I find that a gas grill is best for quick grilling because you can heat it up so quickly, and a Big Green Egg (or charcoal grill, or smoker) is best for slow-smoked meats with natural wood flavors. I also have a wood burning oven outside that I use for cooking things at high temperatures, such as pizza (at 800 degrees F), and meats and fish (at 400 to 500 degrees F).

My favorite cooking pan is one of my many sizes of cast-iron pans. The largest US manufacturer is Loge, made in Tennessee; and they make many different sizes. They recently came out with a lighter weight line that you may like.

Fresh Produce

Having a great garden at home has encouraged me to eat more greens and to use a dehydrator to dry my own herbs. I use dried oregano, rosemary, parsley, and thyme regularly—all easy to grow at home—as well as fresh mint for daily cocktails. We cooked through late winter and then spring during the quarantine. So we began harvesting lettuces and other greens, including red leaf, Boston, bibb, and Romaine, as well as kale and turnips. As spring ensued, we cooked with early vegetables such as zucchini and squash. We were happy to always have plentiful herbs throughout the quarantine.

A day without Wine is a day without Sunshine

A glass of wine is a great addition to any meal, except maybe breakfast. I tend to prefer red, particularly European wines, although my wine affection runs the gamut towards all geographies and varieties, whether white or red. I don't believe in the rule that white wine goes with fish, and red wines should pair with meat; hence, I drink both with all types of cuisine. As far as enhancing food, lighter wines—whether white or light reds—tend to do better with lighter foods, such as fish or chicken. I truly believe that THERE ARE NO RULES. Whatever grabs you is what you should do.

As an intro to wine labels, European wines are generally named by their locale, like Burgundy, Bordeaux, Cote du Rhone, Rioja, Brunello, and others, while US wines and other "new world" wines are named for their grape variety, such as chardonnay, sauvignon blanc, grenache, syrah, pinot noir, cabernet, etc. Look for labels in the recipes to see what I pair with dishes.

SE France, mostly Grenache

California, Cabernet Franc

Oregon, Pinot

Tuscany, south of Florence, Sangiovese

White Burgundy, Chard

Loire Valley, Cab Franc

Central/coastal California, Syrah

France, Burgundy, Pinot

France, Chateauneuf du Pape

Appetizers

GROUPER CEVICHE

SNAPPER CEVICHE

LOBSTER AND SNAPPER CEVICHE

HUMMUS / TAHINI

TABOULEH

GUACAMOLE

AVOCADO TOAST

COLOSSAL SHRIMP

FOCACCIA

PITA BREAD

BEEF SLIDERS

CURED SALMON (LOX)

17

GROUPER CEVICHE

YIELD: 4 to 6
COOK TIME: 30 minutes, plus marinating time

---

1 pound grouper fillet, skin removed, cut into ¼-inch pieces
Juice of 1 lime
Juice of 1 lemon
1 jalapeño, diced, and seeds removed
½ red pepper, diced
½ yellow pepper, diced
½ red onion, diced
1 to 2 cloves garlic, finely diced
⅛ teaspoon cumin
⅛ teaspoon red pepper
Salt, to taste
Cilantro, for garnish
Extra-virgin olive oil, to drizzle

Place the fish pieces in a serving bowl, and toss gently with the lemon and lime juice.

In a separate bowl, mix together the jalapeño, red and yellow peppers, red onion, garlic, cumin, red pepper, and salt to taste. Add these to the bowl of fish, and toss gently to combine. Refrigerate for at least 1 hour, or up to 24 hours before serving.

Serve slightly chilled or at room temperature, topped with cilantro and a drizzle of extra-virgin olive oil.

Ceviche is very easy to make and always a big hit with our guests. It is widely available in European cuisine, particularly Spanish—It's said that its origin is Peru. It is typically made with fresh raw fish or shellfish, combined with fresh citrus, lemon or lime juice, and spiced with chopped onions, and a little heat, such as chili peppers. I use a firm white fish like mahi-mahi or halibut, shrimp, and/or scallops. Ceviche always goes well with chopped fresh avocado and a sprinkle of orange juice. It is great paired with a cold, crisp white wine, like a Burgundy/Chardonnay, or a sparkling wine such as Prosecco or Champagne.

The wine in this photo is "the other white Burgundy." Most white Burgundies are made with Chardonnay grapes, while this white Burgundy is made with Aligoté grape. It is a more acidic grape than Chardonnay, and is described as light and citrusy. It is a great combination for pairing with Ceviche.

SNAPPER CEVICHE

YIELD: 4 servings
COOK TIME: 30 minutes, plus marinating time

½ red onion, diced
½ bell pepper (red, yellow, green, or a combination), diced
½ tomato, chopped
1 jalapeño pepper, diced finely

8 to 12-ounce snapper fillet, cut into ¼-inch cubes
Juice of 1 lime
1 tablespoon extra-virgin olive oil
¼ teaspoon salt
⅛ teaspoon black pepper

Mix the red onions, peppers, tomatoes, jalapeños, and fish cubes in a big bowl. Stir in the lime juice and the olive oil. Season with salt and pepper to taste.
 Stir, cover, and refrigerate for at least 1 hour, or overnight.
 Serve slightly chilled, or at room temperature.

LOBSTER & SNAPPER CEVICHE

YIELD: 4 to 6 servings
COOK TIME: 30 minutes, plus marinating time

½ red onion, diced
½ bell pepper (red, yellow, or green, or combination of colors)
½ tomato, chopped
1 jalapeño pepper, finely diced
1 (8-ounce) snapper fillet, cut into ¼-inch cubes
8 ounces raw lobster claw, cut into ¼-inch cubes
Juice of 1 lime
1 tablespoon extra-virgin olive oil
¼ teaspoon salt
⅛ teaspoon black pepper

Combine the red onions, peppers, tomatoes, jalapeños and fish cubes in a big bowl. Stir in the lime juice, add the extra-virgin olive oil, and mix thoroughly. Season with salt and pepper to taste.
  Stir and refrigerate for at least 1 hour, or overnight.
  Serve slightly chilled, or at room temperature.

HUMMUS/TAHINI

YIELD: 3 cups
COOK TIME: 3 hours

---

1 cup dried chickpeas, or garbanzo beans
2 teaspoons baking soda
1 cup sesame tahini
Juice from 1½ lemons, about ⅓ cup
2 to 4 cloves garlic, finely minced or grated

Salt to taste
½ teaspoon cumin
⅓ to ⅔ cup ice water
Extra-virgin olive oil
Chopped parsley

Soak the chickpeas overnight in enough water to cover. The next day, drain and cover chickpeas with water, stir in the baking soda, and simmer on low heat for 1 to 1½ hours, or until the peas are tender. (For a fast soak the same day you want to cook, bring the beans to a boil, turn off the heat, and let the pot sit, covered, for 1 hour; then drain. Once drained, start the cooking process above.)

While the chickpeas are cooking, mix the tahini sauce, lemon juice, garlic, salt, cumin, and sesame tahini in a medium bowl.

Drain the tender chickpeas and combine with the ingredients in the bowl.

Place the chickpeas in a blender, and slowly add enough iced water until the hummus is perfectly smooth.

Serve topped with a splash of extra-virgin olive oil, or garnished with chopped parsley.

TABOULEH

YIELD: 8 cups
COOK TIME: 45 minutes

½ cup bulgur wheat
1¼ cups water
4 cups fresh parsley, chopped, and divided
1½ cups tomatoes, chopped
¼ cup green onions, just white part, diced

¼ to ½ cup mint, chopped
¼ cup lemon juice
¼ teaspoon garlic, minced
Pinch of salt
1 tablespoon extra-virgin olive oil

In a medium saucepan over high heat, add the bulgur wheat and water and bring just to a boil; then turn off the heat and let the pan sit for 20 to 25 minutes.
  Strain out the liquid and let the wheat cool.
  For a dressing, combine 2 cups parsley, the tomatoes, green onions, and mint in a small bowl.
  In a larger bowl, mix the remaining 2 cups parsley, lemon juice, garlic, salt, and extra-virgin olive oil. Add the cooled bulgur wheat and mix 'til completely blended.
  Serve immediately at room temperature or refrigerate and serve cool. It will keep, refrigerated, for 1 or 2 days.

GUACAMOLE

Avocado is the main ingredient in guacamole, and this simple dish goes well with a lot of different things. It is also great for breakfast spread on toasted bread, with a fried egg on top; in sandwiches with cheese, sprouts and tomatoes; or as an appetizer with chips and Mexican salsa.

YIELD: 2 cups
COOK TIME: 15 minutes

---

1 large ripe avocado
1 tablespoon lime juice
½ onion, finely chopped
½ fresh tomato, finely chopped

1 tablespoon extra-virgin olive oil
1 tablespoon chopped fresh cilantro
½ teaspoon kosher salt

Cut the avocado in half, remove the pit, scoop the meat out and place in a medium bowl. Use a fork to mash 'til smooth. Add the lime juice, onion, tomato, olive oil, and cilantro, and blend together 'til smooth. Sprinkle with kosher salt.

  This can be served immediately, or kept refrigerated for 2 to 3 days.

AVOCADO TOAST

YIELD: 2 servings
COOK TIME: 15 minutes

---

2 slices bread
1 avocado, mashed

2 poached or fried eggs, optional
Salt and pepper to taste

Toast the bread and spread the ripe, mashed avocado atop it.
  If you like, add a poached or fried egg on top of the avocado. Sprinkle with salt and pepper to taste and serve warm or hot.

COLOSSAL SHRIMP

YIELD: 2 to 4 servings
COOK TIME: 5 to 10 minutes, plus marinade time

---

1 pound fresh, extra-large/colossal shrimp (10 to 12 per pound), peeled, tail on
¼ cup extra-virgin olive oil

4 cloves garlic, diced
1 teaspoon salt
½ teaspoon pepper, red or black

In a large bowl combine the oil, garlic, salt, and pepper. Add the shrimp and mix thoroughly in the marinade. Cover and refrigerate for 30 minutes.

Grill the shrimp on high heat on a gas, butane, or wood-burning grill for 5 to 10 minutes, or until they turn pink, turning once to add grill marks.

Do not overcook: shrimp will continue to cook after being removed from the grill.

Serve immediately.

> Colossal, or Jumbo Shrimp (also called "grilling shrimp"), are about 10 shrimp to the pound, with or without the head, but with shells on. I cook them with heads and shells removed, although I do like to leave the tail shell for visual enhancement when serving. Ranging from 8 to 12 shrimp per pound, they are very meaty and filling, loaded with both texture and flavor. They work well as an appetizer, a main course, or added to other dishes like Grilled Shrimp Soup (one of our wonderful leftover lunch meals), or a cold tossed salad. Their uniqueness is their size, flavor, and meatiness. They are generally not local in the southeast or southwest; they often come from places like Argentina or Thailand—places with deeper, colder waters.

FOCACCIA

YIELD: 4 to 6 servings
COOK TIME: 3 hours, including rise time

1 package active dry yeast
5 cups all-purpose flour
1 tablespoon sugar
1 tablespoon salt
½ cup extra-virgin olive oil, for the dough, plus ½ cup extra-virgin olive oil, for coating the pan

Mix the yeast in ¾ cup warm (105 to 115 degrees F) water and let stand 5 minutes until foamy.
 Combine the flour, sugar, salt, and ½ cup olive oil in a blender with a dough hook. Add the yeast mixture and blend together.
 Transfer the dough to a dry surface sprinkled with flour, and knead 1 to 2 times.
 Place the dough in a lightly oiled, medium bowl. Sprinkle with flour, cover with a towel, and let rise until doubled in size, about 1 hour.
 Spread ½ cup olive oil over a jelly roll pan, or small cookie sheet.
 Spread the dough over the entire sheet, pushing it flat against all sides of pan and into the edges. Turn it and coat the other side with oil. Let it rise until it doubles in size, about 1 hour.
 Preheat the oven to 425 degrees F.
 You can decorate the dough any way that grabs you (e.g., cover with thinly sliced vegetables or sprinkle with salt or other seeds, as you wish) just before cooking.
 Place the pan on the middle rack of the oven and bake for 25 to 30 minutes, or until slightly browned.
 Remove the tray to cool on a wired/mesh rack. Serve warm or at room temperature. The focaccia will be good for a day or two, although it is best served warm, straight out of the oven.

PITA BREAD

YIELD: Serves 4
COOK TIME: 2½ hours, including rise time

½ teaspoon active dry yeast
2 teaspoons sugar
2 cups all-purpose flour
2 cups bread flour
1½ teaspoon salt
2 tablespoons extra-virgin olive oil

In a small bowl, combine the yeast with ½ cup warm water (105 to 115 degrees), and let stand about 5 minutes, or until foamy.
 In a medium bowl, combine the sugar, both flours, and the salt; then add the yeast mixture.
 In a mixer, blend the dough with an additional ½ cup water and the olive oil, until the dough comes together and starts to pull clear of the bowl. At that point, add another ½ cup water and continue to blend.
 Cover the bowl with a towel and let the dough rise 1 hour, or until it doubles in size.
 Divide the mixture into 8 balls. Cover the bowl with the balls in it with plastic and let them rise until they are the size of softballs, about 1 hour.
 Preheat the oven to 500 degrees F.
 Roll out each ball of dough to ¼-inch-thick discs. Place 1 or 2 at a time on a baking stone, or an inverted baking sheet, and bake on the upper third portion of the oven for 3 minutes, or until the bread has puffed up.
 Serve hot immediately, or cool to room temperature and serve later. These will keep in the refrigerator up to one week.

FOCACCIA VS PITA BREAD

Focaccia and Pita Bread are both flatbreads, very similar in ingredients, but from two different countries and cultures. Focaccia is Italian, while Pita is Middle Eastern. Other flatbreads and their countries of origin include Chapati/Indian, Lavash/Armenian, and Tortillas/Mexican, to name a few. Pizza dough is another flatbread. They are used for a variety of dishes including wraps (tortillas), pockets (pita), pizza-like flatbread dishes with many different toppings.

BEEF SLIDERS

This slider is shown with tomatoes and cheese, but feel free to add whatever extras you like on your burgers. Sliders can be prepared with a variety of meats but are best with a mixture of chuck and brisket, if they're to be beef. It's important that they have a little extra fat, like brisket or even pork, to make the overall flavor juicier. In addition, they're really great if they're cooked on a flat griddle, or a cast-iron skillet. This way they cook in their own juices/fats. Of course, you can cook them on a hot grill, if you prefer a crispy finish. I recommend a mixture of 75% chuck and 25% brisket. So, if you go to the butcher, ask him to mix ¾ pound of chuck and ¼ pound of brisket to make 4-ounce patties. This makes an oversized slider (a typical slider can be 2 to 3 ounces), or a smallish burger for a main course. Feel free to experiment with the blend. You can even try lamb or pork. Sliders make great appetizers and lunch dishes. Of course, they can also be enlarged into full-sized 8-ounce burgers for a complete meal.

YIELD: 4 servings
COOK TIME: 20 minutes

---

8 ounces ground chuck
8 ounces ground brisket
4 brioche buns

Cook the meat patties on a griddle at high heat for 2 to 3 minutes per side until done to your liking, but do not overcook. Remove from the grill and set aside to rest for 5 minutes.

Reduce the griddle heat to medium and warm the insides of the buns for 2 minutes.

Assemble the sliders with whatever extras you like, and serve hot.

HOW-TO CURE SALMON

I grew up eating bagels and lox, generally non-salty Nova lox. But once I learned this recipe at a cooking class, it was so easy and wonderfully tender, I began making it as an appetizer for dinners, or with a bagel and cream cheese for breakfast. This is one of my staples that I like to have around in the refrigerator. It will keep for a week or more there.

Salmon can be embellished with all sorts of flavors, such as vanilla, vodka, citrus zest, or candied citrus for a more traditional gravlax. Twenty-four hours is a minimum curing period, but if you prefer it more dried-out, it can be cured for 36 to 48 hours. It will drain all of the liquid out of the fish, so don't be surprised to see a brownish liquid on the pan when you take it out of the refrigerator. The basics are salt and sugar.

Wrap the fish in plastic and foil, then weight it down with an iron skillet during curing.

CURED SALMON (LOX)

I tend to like Atlantic Salmon, most of which is farm-raised. I prefer it to a wild salmon because it has more fat and is soft and tender, although you can certainly use a wild Coho or King River salmon.

YIELD: 10 servings
COOK TIME: 30 minutes to prep, 24 to 36 hours to cure

- 3 tablespoons ground coriander seed
- 2 tablespoons ground fennel seed
- 2 tablespoons ground caraway seed
- 2 tablespoons whole pepper, ground
- 1 tablespoon mustard powder
- 1 tablespoon dried thyme
- ½ cup finely chopped fresh dill, or fennel fronds
- 2 tablespoons minced garlic
- 2 tablespoons minced shallots
- ¾ cup kosher salt
- 1¾ cups brown sugar
- 1 pound salmon, fresh Atlantic farm-raised, skin-on, deboned, and rinsed
- 2 tablespoons fennel fronds and/or fresh parsley, chopped

In a small bowl, mix the coriander, fennel, caraway, and whole pepper.

Add the herbs to a large bowl, along with the mustard and thyme. Toss with the minced shallots and garlic and add the salt and sugar.

Lay the salmon skin-side down on a large cookie sheet, spread the brine evenly over the meat side, patting it on to cover well, and wrap tightly with plastic wrap; then cover with aluminum foil.

Place the salmon in the refrigerator and place a cookie sheet or pan over the fish. Place heavy cans or a caste iron skillet atop the cookie sheet to weight it down. This will press the brine into the flesh. Refrigerate for 24 to 36 hours.

Wash all brine off the fish when done, and pat dry. Dust with the fresh dill or fennel fronds.

Use a sharp knife, such as a tomato knife, to slice on a bias as thinly as possible.

Serve cold with your favorite accompaniments (e.g., chopped hard boiled eggs, capers, minced red onions, crème fresh, yogurt, sour cream) on a bagel or toast points. Garnish with chopped parsley.

Salads & Soup

CAESAR SALAD
GRILLED CAESER
ARUGULA SALAD
CUCUMBER, TOMATO, & FETA SALAD
BEET & AVOCADO SALAD
SIMPLE GREEN SALAD WITH VINAIGRETTE
CHICKEN STOCK
CHICKEN NOODLE SOUP
ANDOUILLE & CHICKEN GUMBO
ITALIAN BEAN SOUP
GRILLED SHRIMP SOUP
MUSHROOM & BARLEY SOUP
CAULIFLOWER & GINGER SOUP
TURKEY CHILI
WHITE BEAN & SPINACH SOUP
CHOPPED SALAD

CAESAR SALAD

I learned to make this many years ago at Nino's, an old-line Atlanta Italian restaurant. The owner, Tony, was a gregarious restaurateur who had great pride in serving it at the table. It used to be that top-end restaurants would always make them at the table, all the ingredients mixed carefully in a large wooden bowl with two forks. I make Caeser salads regularly. In fact, when Robin was pregnant with Andy, our son, she craved Caesars. As a very young child, Andy loved them too, particularly the anchovies. To this day, both he and Robin love Caesar Salads. While it's traditional to add croutons, we prefer the salad without. It's a bit lighter, a little simpler to make, and less filling. We save the calories for really good bread or other carbohydrates.

YIELD: Serves 4 to 6
COOK TIME: 15 minutes

---

1 head Romaine lettuce, roughly chopped	½ teaspoon Dijon mustard
Juice of ½ lemon	1 egg yolk
1 teaspoon salt	¼ cup red wine vinegar
2 to 3 cloves garlic	½ cup of extra-virgin olive oil
2 to 3 anchovy fillets, canned in olive oil	¼ cup grated or shaved Parmesan cheese
½ teaspoon Worcestershire sauce	1 teaspoon freshly ground pepper

---

Wrap the chopped Romaine in a paper towel, put it in a bowl, cover, and refrigerate at least ½ hour to crisp.

In a big wooden bowl, add the salt and lemon juice. (This will provide grit in the wooden bowl to create the salad dressing.)

In the same bowl, use two forks to crush and grind the garlic and the anchovy fillets, to create a paste for the salad dressing. Feel free to use a little of the oil from the can to add flavor. Stir the Worcestershire sauce, mustard, and egg yolk into the paste. Add the vinegar and oil, in a 1:2 ratio and mix until smooth, stirring constantly as you drizzle the oil and vinegar into the bowl. Taste and correct the seasonings with salt and pepper.

Toss the Romaine lettuce in the wooden bowl and coat with the salad dressing.

Dust the salad with Parmesan cheese, add freshly ground pepper to taste, and serve.

GRILLED CAESAR SALAD

YIELD: 2 servings
COOK TIME: 15 minutes

---

1 head Romaine lettuce
Extra-virgin olive oil, or canola oil spray
½ cup Caesar dressing (recipe, page 34)

Cut the entire head of lettuce in half lengthwise, leaving the bottom leaves attached to hold together. Spray the lettuce, the leaves, and the bottom with oil and then grill to a char, about 2 minutes on each side.
Once grilled, drizzle Caesar dressing onto the leaves, and serve immediately while still warm.

ARUGULA SALAD

YIELD: 2 to 4 servings
COOK TIME: 10 minutes

---

16 ounces arugula, whole leaves
2 ounces Parmesan cheese, sliced or shaved
Juice of 1 lemon
¼ cup extra-virgin olive oil
Salt and pepper to taste

Add the shaved Parmesan to a bowl with the fresh arugula. Toss with the lemon juice and olive oil. Sprinkle with salt and pepper to taste.

Buy whole Parmesan cheese for the best taste. I use a peeler or a cheese knife to slice the cheese into large flakes, or grate if you prefer. I also added multi-colored beets and goat cheese to this salad, although the Arugula Salad is just as great with a simple lemon/oil drizzle and shaved Parmesan.

CUCUMBER, TOMATO & FETA SALAD

YIELD: 4 servings
COOK TIME: 15 minutes, plus marinade time

---

1 cucumber, halved, cored, seeded and cubed
1 tomato, cored and cubed
4 ounces feta cheese, cubed
⅛ cup red wine vinegar
¼ cup extra-virgin olive oil
Salt and pepper to taste

In a medium bowl, toss the cubes of cucumber, tomato, and feta with the red wine vinegar and extra-virgin olive oil. Add salt and pepper to taste, cover, and refrigerate at least 30 minutes before you serve. You can also add it to a bed of chopped Romaine (as above) for a great variation.

BEET & AVOCADO SALAD

YIELD: 2 servings
COOK TIME: 20 to 30 minutes, plus time to cook the beets

---

1 beet, red and/or yellow, precooked, and cubed
1 avocado, cubed
1 tomato, cored and cubed
⅛ cup vinegar, red wine, or champagne
Juice of ½ lemon
¼ cup extra-virgin olive oil

Preheat the oven to 400 degrees F. Wash and rinse the beet, wrap in foil, and bake for 1 hour. Unwrap while still hot and peel off the skin by hand under running water. Use a peeler to remove the skin that can't be rubbed off. Cube and refrigerate for 30 minutes to chill, or keep refrigerated up to 1 week. When the beet has chilled, toss it in a bowl with the avocado, tomato, vinegar, and lemon juice. Slowly add the oil in a drizzle as you continue to toss, and serve at room temperature or chilled.

SIMPLE GREEN SALAD
WITH VINAIGRETTE

The ratio of vinegar to oil is almost always 1:2 for a good dressing. For a more complex vinaigrette, you can add a little lemon, mustard, or fruit jelly. One of my favorite things to do is whisk blue cheese into the dressing to make it creamy.

YIELD: 2 servings
COOK TIME: 15 minutes

---

1 cup torn or chopped lettuces: red and green Romaine, bibb, arugula, or spinach
⅛ cup vinegar (champagne or red wine)
1 teaspoon salt

¼ cup extra-virgin olive oil
Salt and pepper to taste

Cut or tear all lettuces into bite-sized pieces; then rinse, and wrap in a paper towel to dry. Put into a bowl and refrigerate to crisp while you are preparing the dressing.

In a small or medium bowl, add the vinegar, then slowly whisk the oil into the bowl for 2 or 3 minutes until all the oil has been added, and the dressing is well combined.

Place the chilled lettuces in a serving bowl and toss with the vinaigrette.

CHICKEN STOCK

YIELD: 12 cups
COOK TIME: 1 to 2 hours

> Quick Tip: The cooked chicken can be pulled off the bones and shredded or chopped for use in the soup, or even for a chicken salad.

1 whole chicken, rinsed
12 cups water
1 stalk celery, cut into 2 to 3 pieces
1 onion, quartered
1 carrot, cut into 3 pieces
2 to 3 bay leaves
1 whole clove garlic, peeled
2 tablespoons salt
1 tablespoon whole peppercorns

Place the whole chicken in a large stock pot and fill with water. Add celery, onion, carrots, bay leaves, garlic, salt, and peppercorns. Cover and simmer on medium-low heat for 1 to 2 hours.

Drain the chicken stock into a lidded pot, setting aside the chicken and carrots to use in soup. Let the stock cool to room temperature, cover, and refrigerate overnight.

The next day, skim the fat off the top and strain the stock into a container. Refrigerate, and use within 1 week, or freeze for up to 6 months. You can use as a liquid to enrich many different recipes.

CHICKEN NOODLE SOUP

YIELD: 4 servings
COOK TIME: 30 minutes

8 ounces noodles (whole wheat spaghetti or angel hair)
2 tablespoons extra-virgin olive oil
1 carrot, chopped
1 celery, chopped
1 onion, diced
1 garlic, minced
8 ounces chicken, white and/or dark meat, raw and deboned, diced
4 to 6 cups chicken stock (recipe above)
Salt and pepper to taste
2 tablespoons chopped parsley

Cook the noodles according to package directions. Drain and set aside.

Add the olive oil to a medium stockpot over medium heat and sauté the carrots, celery, onion, and garlic about 5 minutes until translucent.

Add the raw diced chicken to the pot and cook for 5 minutes. Add the chicken stock and simmer for 15 minutes to blend the tastes.

Add the noodles, and simmer for 5 minutes to warm them.

Add salt and pepper to taste, top with parsley, and serve hot.

There is nothing better than fresh, homemade stock for soups, be it chicken, beef, vegetable, or seafood. I like to have it handy, fresh or frozen, at all times. It is great to use in many other dishes, including stir-fry dishes, rice, and pasta dishes, to name a few. I make stock regularly using a whole chicken cut into four parts. Sometimes I cut the meat off the breasts, thighs, and legs from the carcass before making a stock. Then I save the meat for other dishes and use the remaining bones, made up of the backbone and the wings, for the stock. I hear that a great stock can be had from just chicken wings. This will make a thinner stock, but it's still good. When I use the whole chicken, I carefully pull the meat off the carcass after making the stock and re-use it in a soup or stew.

ANDOUILLE & CHICKEN GUMBO

Gumbo is the official state cuisine of Louisiana. Gumbo is also a generic term used in Louisiana to refer to the mixing of many different things, be it food or people—the melting pot of populations that make up Louisiana, and its Creole and Cajun descendants. Everyone makes Gumbo differently, but there are basics. The roux is the base, the sauce that thickens the soup. The vegetables are the traditional holy trinity: celery, onions, and bell peppers. After that, it's up to the chef. In central Louisiana it's served with chopped boiled eggs, but mostly it's served with rice. Generally not a vegetarian soup, gumbo contains chicken, with or without sausage, or fish and/or shellfish. Anything goes. As they say in Louisiana, "Laissez les bon temps rouler"—let the good times roll!

YIELD: 4 to 6 cups
COOK TIME: 1 hour

---

1 cup cooked rice	8 cups chicken stock, or water
½ cup canola, grapeseed, or peanut oil	8 ounces chicken, raw and diced
½ cup all-purpose flour	8 ounces andouille sausage, cut in
1 stalk celery, coarsely chopped	1 to 2-inch slices
1 green pepper, coarsely chopped	1 tablespoon hot Cajun spice (I like to use
1 onion, coarsely chopped	Slap Yo Mamma brand)

Cook the rice according to package instructions and set-aside.

Heat the oil in a big stockpot on medium heat, and add the flour slowly, a small bit at a time. Cook, stirring constantly, until the roux is a nutty brown. This takes patience, and will take 30 minutes or more. DON'T OVERCOOK OR BURN THE FLOUR.

Add the celery, green pepper, and onions, and cook for 3 to 5 minutes. Lower the heat to medium-low, add the chicken stock (or water), then the chicken and andouille sausage. Season with Slap Yo Mamma (or your favorite hot Cajun spice), bring to a simmer, and simmer for 15 minutes, or until the meat is cooked through.

Serve with 1 or 2 tablespoons of rice per bowl, and a Chopped Salad (recipe, page 49).

ITALIAN BEAN SOUP

YIELD: 6 to 8 servings
COOK TIME: 30 to 45 minutes

---

2 tablespoons extra-virgin olive oil
½ red, green or yellow pepper, coarsely chopped
½ onion, coarsely chopped
2 ounces (about 4) shiitake mushrooms, sliced
8 ounces greens, kale, or spinach, chopped
12 cups chicken or vegetable stock, or water
1 (12-ounce) can Italian beans, or use dried and pre-soaked beans
4 ounces cooked chicken, shredded or cubed
1 tablespoon salt
1 teaspoon ground pepper

Add the olive oil to a medium to large stockpot over medium heat, and sauté the peppers, onions, mushrooms, and greens for 5 minutes, or until they are translucent and soft, but not overcooked.

Add the stock and beans to the vegetables.

Stir in the chicken, and cook on low heat for at least 30 minutes, or until the beans are cooked and the flavors have blended. You can't overcook this soup, but it will become mushy. It's a matter of preference.

Feel free to be creative and use another leftover meat you like instead of chicken, or just leave the protein out and make this a vegetarian soup.

GRILLED SHRIMP SOUP

YIELD: 4 to 6 servings
COOK TIME: 30 minutes

> Hot Tip: This was one of our "happy mistakes" during quarantine. It's a great way to use left-over grilled shrimp!

SHRIMP STOCK
Shells from 1 pound colossal shrimp
8 cups water
1 tablespoon salt
1 tablespoon peppercorns

SOUP
1 pound colossal or jumbo shrimp (10 to 12 shrimp per pound size), shelled and deveined
2 tablespoons olive oil
1 carrot, large dice
1 celery, large dice
1 onion, large dice

To make the shrimp stock, shell the shrimp and set the shrimp aside while you make the stock. Boil the shells in 8 cups water, the salt, and peppercorns for about 30 minutes. Strain the stock and save the liquid. Discard the shells.

Grill the colossal shrimp on high heat on a gas, propane, or wood-burning grill for 5 minutes, turning once, until just pink. Don't overcook.

Add the olive oil to a medium stockpot over medium heat, and sauté the carrot, celery, and onion about 5 minutes until translucent.

Add the grilled shrimp and the shrimp stock to the stockpot with the sautéed vegetables, and simmer on low heat for 10 to 15 minutes. Serve immediately.

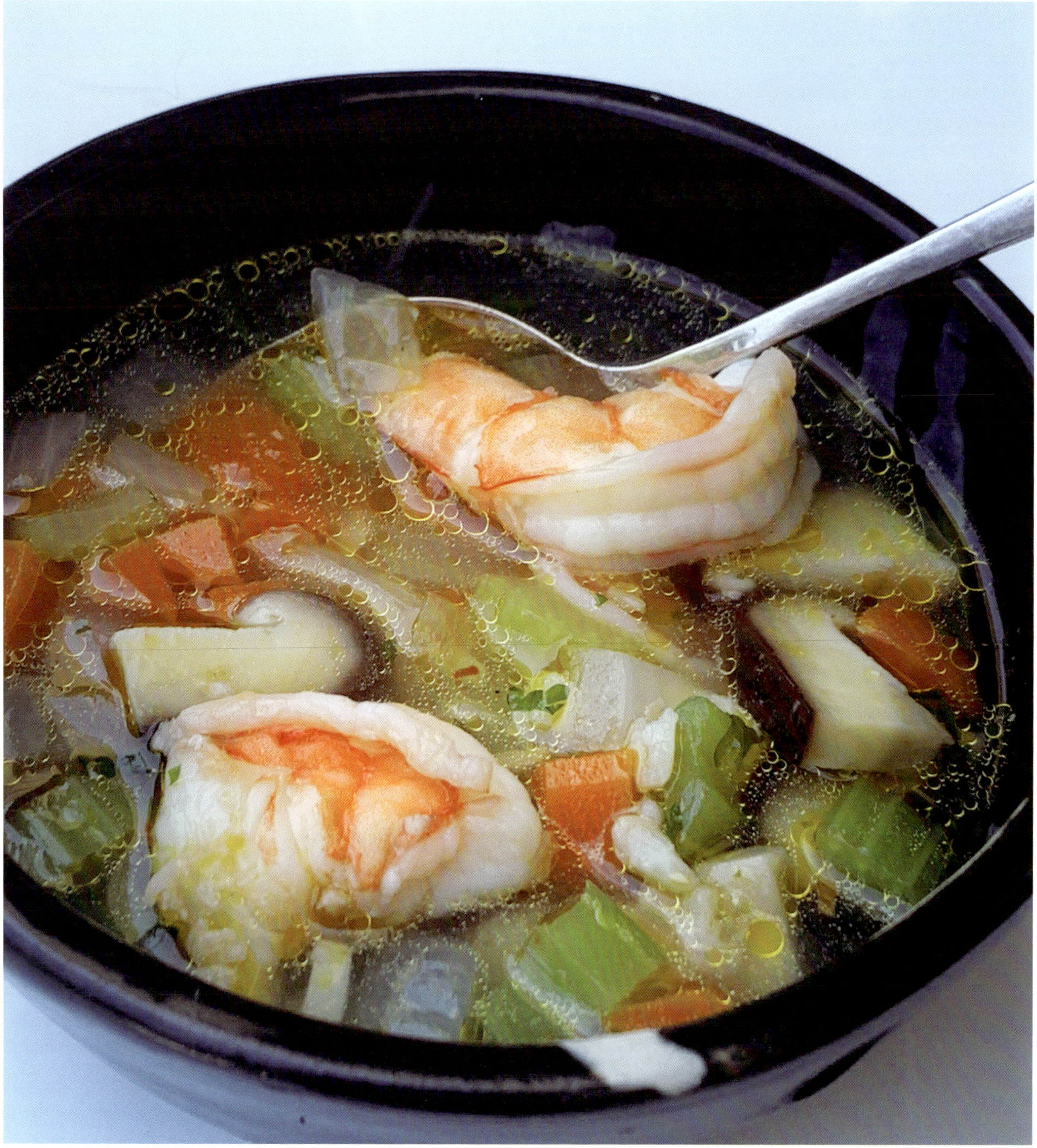

MUSHROOM & BARLEY SOUP

YIELD: 6 to 8 servings
COOK TIME: 1 hour, 15 minutes

---

2 tablespoons olive oil
1 onion, chopped
2 ounces shiitake mushrooms, sliced
2 carrots, chopped
2 stalks celery, chopped

2 cloves garlic, minced
1 cup raw barley
12 cups chicken or vegetable stock, or water
1 tablespoon salt
1 teaspoon ground black pepper

In a stockpot over medium heat, add the olive oil and sauté the onions, shiitake mushrooms, carrots, and celery about 5 minutes until translucent. Add the garlic and saute for 1 minute more. Add the barley and stock, increase the heat to medium-high, and bring just to a boil. Reduce the heat to low, and simmer, uncovered, for 1 hour, stirring occasionally.

  Add salt and pepper to taste, and serve warm.

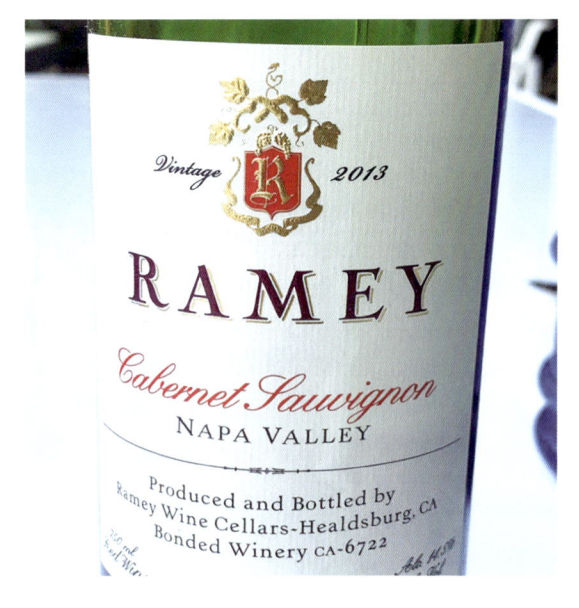

Enjoy your Mushroom & Barley Soup with a hearty cabernet, a full-bodied wine.

CAULIFLOWER & GINGER SOUP

YIELD: 6 servings
COOK TIME: 15 to 20 minutes

---

1 head cauliflower, chopped
4 cups water, or chicken or vegetable stock
1 onion, coarsely chopped
1 carrot, coarsely chopped

1 stalk celery, coarsely chopped
1 tablespoon freshly shredded ginger
¼ cup chopped fresh parsley

Add the cauliflower and water or stock to a stockpot over medium heat; then stir in the onions, carrots, celery, and ginger. Cook uncovered for 15 to 20 minutes, or until the vegetables are tender. Remove from heat and set aside to cool a bit. Then use an immersion blender to mix until smooth. To serve, reheat until hot, and garnish each serving bowl with a tablespoon of parsley.

TURKEY CHILI

YIELD: 6 to 8
COOK TIME: 1 hour, plus time to prepare beans

8 ounces dried beans	12 ounces chicken or vegetable stock, or water
8 ounces dried kidney beans	1 (8-ounce) can tomatoes
2 tablespoons high heat oil, such as grapeseed, canola or peanut oil	1 teaspoon dried oregano
	½ teaspoon cumin
1 onion, chopped	1 tablespoon chili
1 clove garlic, minced	¼ cup shredded cheddar cheese
1 pound ground turkey	¼ cup sour cream

Soak the beans overnight in enough water to cover (or for a fast soak, bring the beans to a boil, turn off the heat, and let the pot sit, covered, for 1 hour; then drain). Alternatively, you can get good organic canned beans at almost any grocery store, which work very well; plus they're already soaked and pre-cooked.

Add the oil to a medium or large stockpot over medium heat, and sauté the onion, garlic, and ground turkey about 10 minutes, or until the turkey is cooked through.

Add the beans and water (or stock), and the tomatoes, sautéed onions, and turkey; then decrease the heat to low, cover, and simmer for 30 to 45 minutes until tender and well blended.

Sprinkle each serving bowl with a tablespoon of cheddar cheese and add a dollop of sour cream.

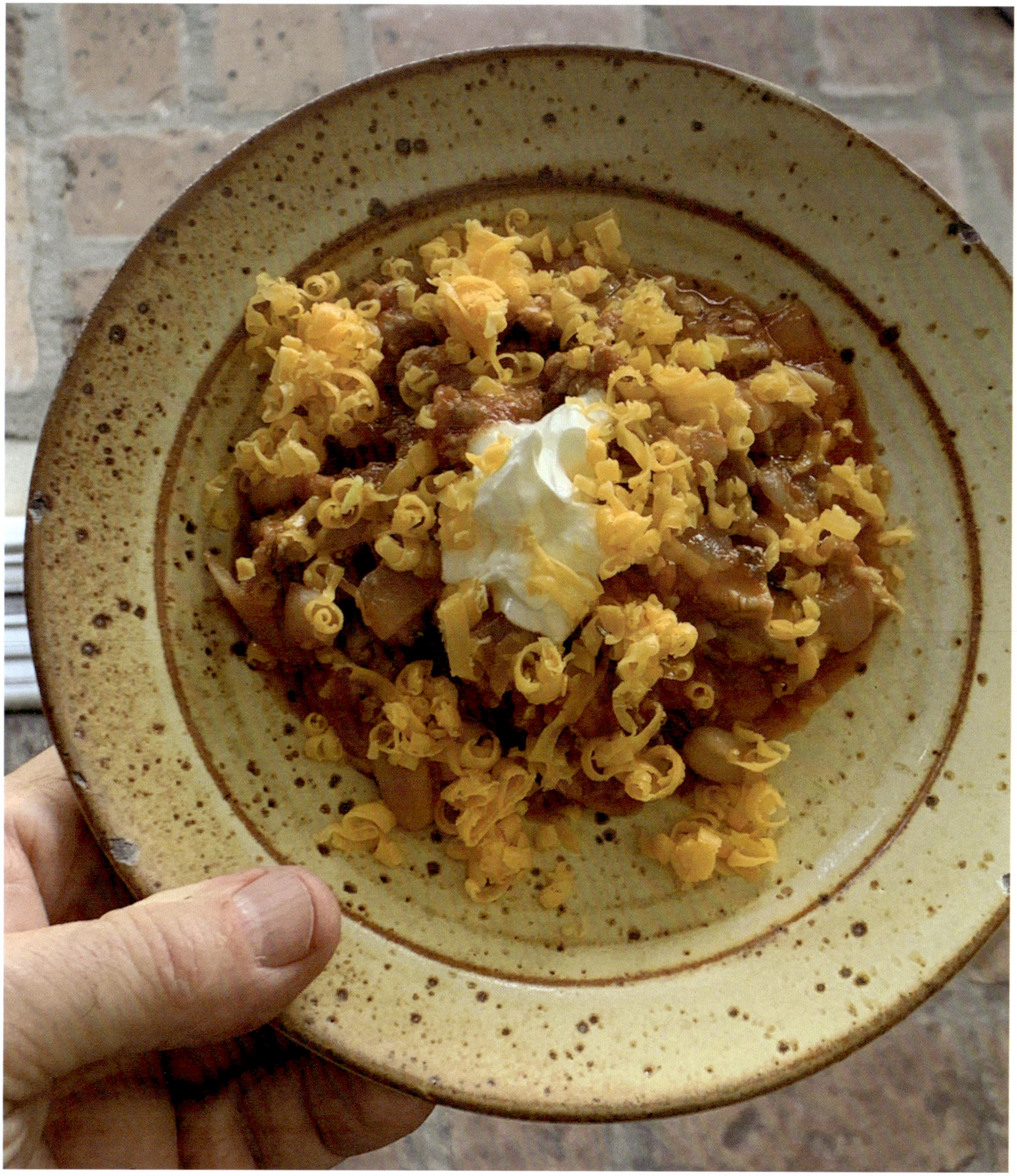

> **Hot Tip:**
> Because dried herbs are more potent than fresh herbs, you need less. The correct ratio is one tablespoon fresh herbs to one teaspoon dried herbs.

WHITE BEAN & SPINACH SOUP

YIELD: 6 servings
COOK TIME: 1 hour

---

2 tablespoons grapeseed, canola, or peanut oil
1 carrot, large dice
1 stalk celery, large dice
1 onion, large dice
1 garlic clove, diced
12 cups chicken or vegetable stock, or water
1 (15-ounce) can white beans, or dried beans soaked overnight, or quick soaked
8 ounces fresh spinach, chopped
1 teaspoon of seasonings of your choice tarragon, oregano, and/or dill (fresh or dried)
1 tablespoon salt
1 teaspoon black pepper

Add the oil to a medium to large stockpot over medium heat and sauté the carrot, celery, onion, and garlic for 5 minutes until translucent.

Add the stock, white beans, spinach, and seasonings, and simmer at medium heat for 30 minutes, or until the beans are tender. If you have used dried beans, you'll need to cook for 1 hour. You can also cook longer on a very low simmer; if the soup gets too thick simply add more liquid.

Season with salt and pepper to taste and serve immediately.

CHOPPED SALAD

YIELD: 4 servings
COOK TIME: 15 minutes

---

8 ounces arugula, chopped
8 ounces Romaine lettuce, chopped
2 ounces (4 to 6) mushrooms, thinly sliced
1 red pepper, thinly sliced
½ red onion, diced
Juice of ½ lemon
2 tablespoons red wine vinegar
1 tablespoon salt, plus more for seasoning
¼ cup extra-virgin olive oil
2 ounces blue cheese, crumbled, optional

In a large salad bowl, combine the lettuces, mushrooms, red pepper, and red onions.

In another small bowl, whisk together the lemon juice, vinegar, and salt; then slowly whisk in the olive oil until blended, and add salt and pepper to taste.

Pour over the salad, add blue cheese crumbles if you like, and toss. Serve immediately.

I really like simple salads with whatever fresh vegetables I have on hand. If I have some fresh cheese like Parmesan, goat cheese, or blue cheese, I'll sprinkle that on the salad as well. Oftentimes, I will simply sprinkle oil and vinegar on top of the finished salad as a dressing and toss it all together to coat. Then I finish with a little salt and pepper. Voila!

Fish

STEAMED MUSSELS IN PASTA

CRAB CAKES WITH GARLIC AIOLI

CRAWFISH BOIL

STONE CRAB CLAWS WITH MUSTARD SAUCE

SAUTÉED GROUPER WITH PEANUT SAUCE

MAHI-MAHI WITH SPINACH AND PASTA

GRILLED SALMON

THAI CHILI SHRIMP

SHRIMP FAJITA WITH CONDIMENTS

GRILLED SHRIMP & SCALLOPS WITH PASTA

GRILLED STRIPED BASS

51

STEAMED MUSSELS IN PASTA

Robin and I really love steamed mussels (with or without steamed clams), and they make for a great lunch or an appetizer for dinner. They tend to be a little too light to make a whole meal, so we generally add something else light to go with them. In this picture you'll see how we combined them—a simple pizza with mushrooms, and a pizza shell lightly coated with tomato sauce and cheese, then topped with some chopped mushrooms. Another great combination is a simple green salad with vinaigrette. You'll also see some toasted baguettes in the background, smeared with butter and lightly sprinkled with powdered garlic and baked in the oven for 10 to 15 minutes at 350 degrees. If they still need browning, broil for 2 to 3 minutes. Be careful not to burn.. These make a wonderful mop for the juices that serve to steam the mussels. All of this goes great with a light, white wine.

SERVES: 4 to 6
COOK TIME: 30 to 40 minutes

1 cup cooked angel hair pasta	½ red bell pepper, chopped
2 tablespoons extra-virgin olive oil	⅛ teaspoon red pepper
½ onion, diced	Water, or chicken stock
1 to 2 cloves garlic, minced	2 tablespoons butter
½ green bell pepper, chopped	2½ pounds mussels, or 1 bag

Cook the pasta according to package directions and set aside. Save 1 cup of pasta water from the pasta pot.

Add the olive oil to a large saucepan over medium heat and sauté the onion, garlic, and green and red peppers for 5 minutes until translucent and soft.

Add 2 to 4 inches of water or chicken stock; increase the heat and bring to boil.

Add the mussels, cover, and steam, still boiling, for 10 to 15 minutes, or until the mussels open. If some of the mussels do not open, just discard them.

Add the cooked pasta and the butter to the mussels. The butter will emulsify, creating a thin silky sauce. If the sauce gets too thick or evaporates too much, just add pasta water to thicken it up. The pasta water serves to add starch to the sauce.

Serve in a shallow bowl, or a large plate with pasta and sauce on the bottom, topped with mussels.

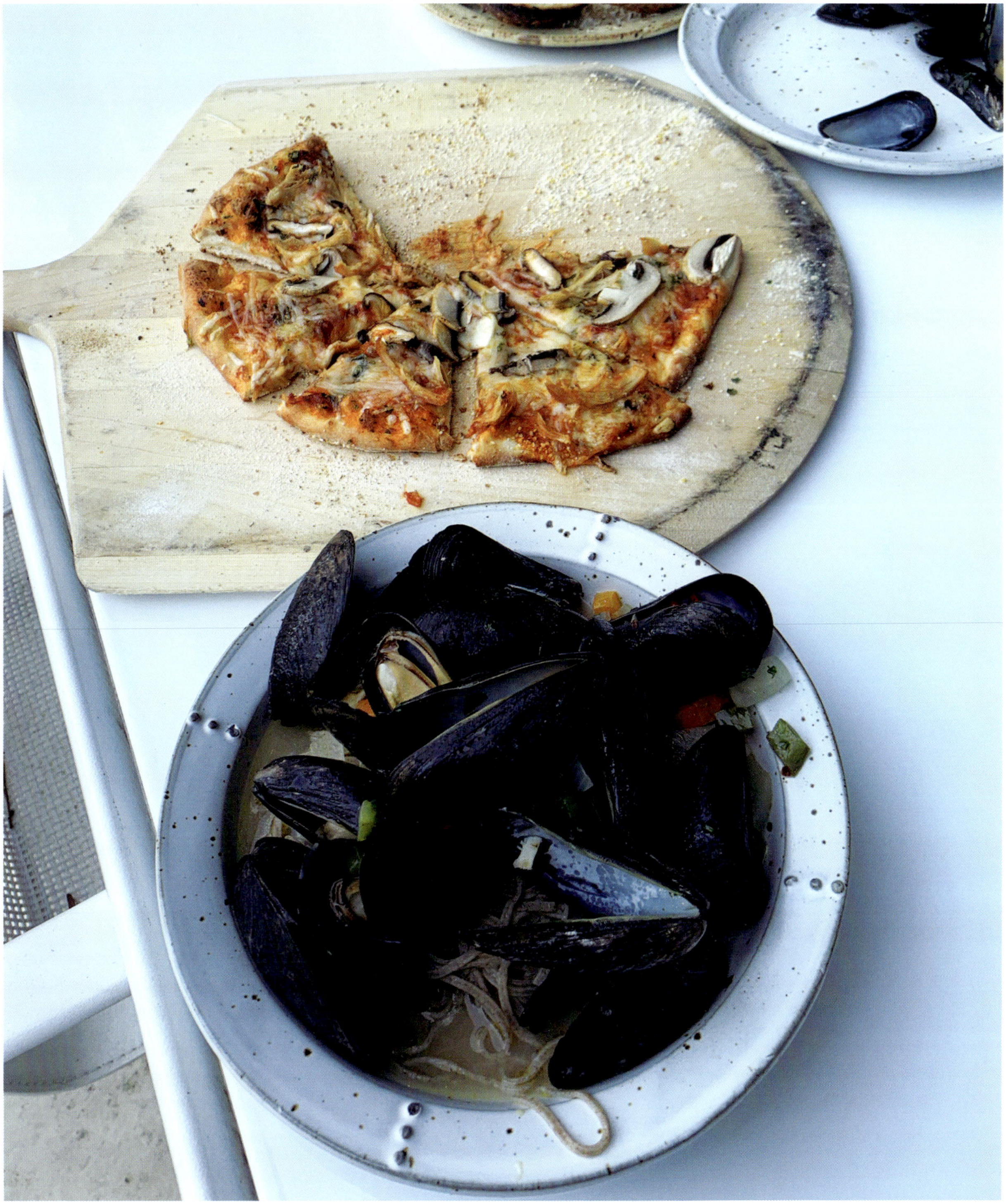

Hot Tip: Crab cakes make a nice, simple lunch. They go great with a crisp, cold white wine, or a light, full-bodied pinot noir (Burgundy). In the photo, you'll see I served the crab cake along with a mini-grill cheese sandwich and some fresh watermelon.

CRAB CAKES

YIELD: 2 crab cakes
COOK TIME: 30 minutes

½ pound crab meat
¼ green pepper, finely diced
¼ yellow onion, finely diced
2 cloves of garlic, finely diced
1 egg white

Juice of ½ lime
2 tablespoons mayonnaise
¼ cup chopped fresh cilantro
1 cup breadcrumbs, or panko
2 tablespoons olive oil

Combine and mix all ingredient thoroughly in a medium bowl.
  Form 2 crab cakes and flatten each into a small, puck-shaped pattie.
  Cook on a griddle on medium heat with 2 tablespoons olive oil, turning to brown each side. They can also be cooked in the oven at 350 degrees for 15 minutes, with a dab of butter on top. If you want to brown more, then simply broil for 5 minutes.
  Serve with garlic aioli (recipe below).

GARLIC AIOLI

YIELD: 2 cups
COOK TIME: 15 minutes

---

2 cloves garlic, finely minced
½ cup sour cream
1 cup mayonnaise

1 tablespoon celery seed
1 lemon, juiced
⅓ cup extra-virgin olive oil

Whisk all the ingredients together in a large bowl for about 5 minutes until well blended. Serve chilled or at room temperature.

CRAWFISH BOIL

How do you eat these? Yes, you need to "suck the head and bite the tail," Cajun style—Squeeze with your thumb at the base of the tail, bite down and squeeze the tail meat out with your teeth. Crawfish season in Louisiana & Mississippi generally runs from November through July, although it's best January through May. You can buy these live, but most purveyors offer them cooked; in which case, you simply warm them up with potatoes, onions, and corn.

YIELD: 2 servings
COOK TIME: 30 minutes

¼ cup Old Bay seasoning
2 ears of corn, cut in half
1 onion, cut into quarters
1 head garlic

2 to 4 small potatoes
5 to 10 pounds fresh gulf coast crawfish (delivered from Inland Seafood)

In a large pot, combine the seasoning, corn, onion, garlic, potatoes, and enough water to cover.

Bring to a boil over high heat, then reduce the heat to medium-low and simmer about 10 minutes, or until the vegetables are fork tender.

Turn off the heat, but leave the pot on the burner, and add the crawfish. After about 10 minutes in the hot water, they will turn red.

Serve immediately. Drain the pot, put lots of newspaper on your table to cover it, and place the drained crawfish and vegetables on top. Add a bowl to the table for shells.

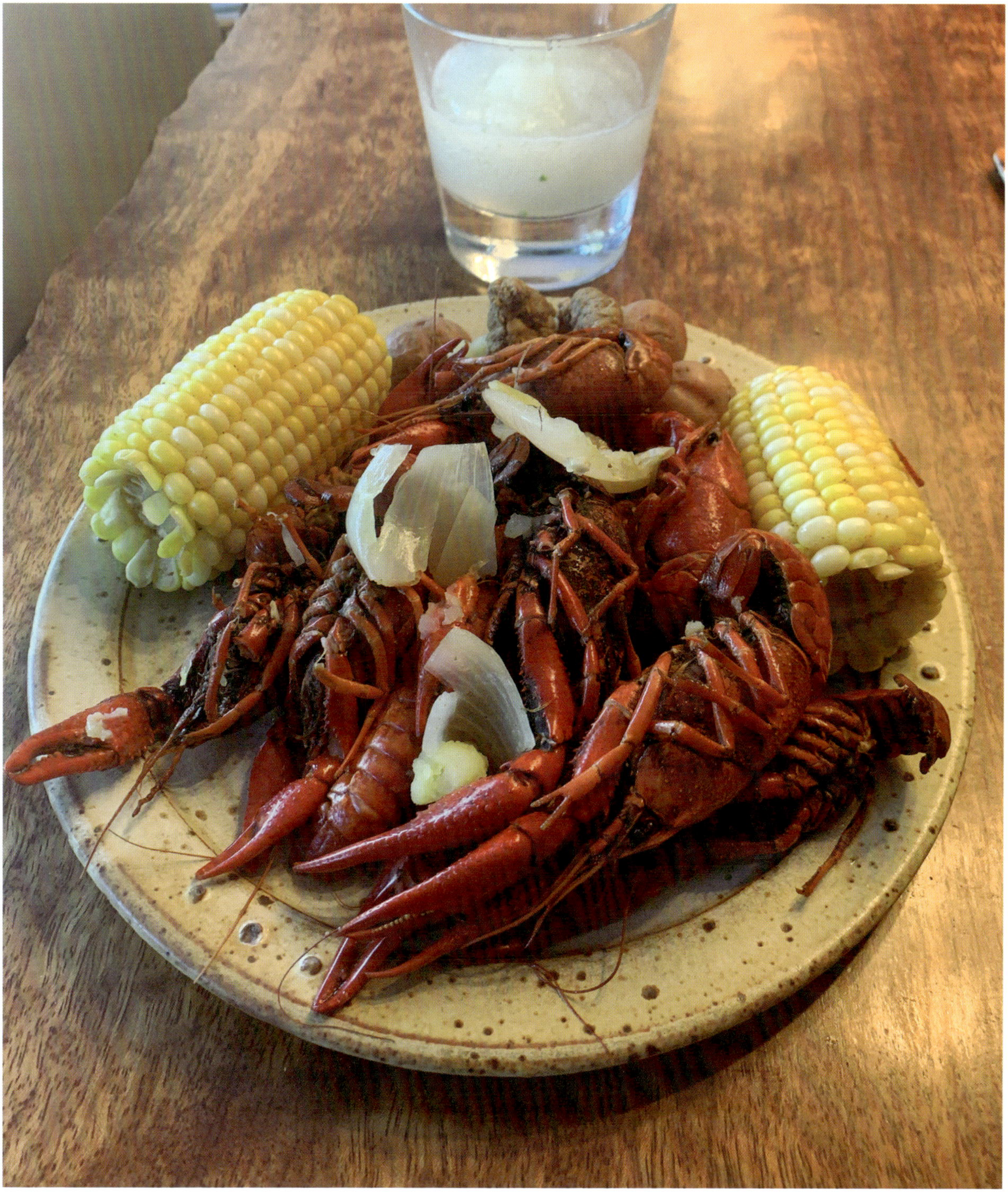

Hot Tip:
Crabs are seasonal from October through May, and they come pre-cooked; they are cooked on the boats that they are caught on, generally in the Gulf of Mexico or near the Caribbean. Most that we get in Atlanta come from South Florida or the Tampa Bay area of Florida.

STONE CRAB CLAWS

These crabs get their name because of their very hard shell. You can place them on a cutting board and use a mallet or a meat tenderizer to crack them. Be sure to crack them thoroughly, or you'll be very frustrated in removing the meat from the claws. Robin says that they can't be cracked enough, as she struggles with the last bits of glorious meat. So, don't under-crack them or you won't be happy! Once well cracked, pull the shell off the meat and dig the meat out with a cocktail fork or a pick. We can't wait for these, since they're very seasonal. We're at the fish market on October 15th at each year. The season lasts until May 15th, although the best claws quit coming after April.

YIELD: 2 servings

---

3 pounds stone crabs
¼ cup Mustard Sauce (recipe below)

1/4 cup melted butter
Juice of 1 lemon

Crack the crabs on a wooden cutting board with a towel placed over them. If you don't cover them when cracking, you'll have an absolute mess. Most places we purchase them from will crack them with a large table-mounted nut cracker, so don't hesitate to ask.

Serve chilled with a pick or a long cocktail fork, a lobster claw cracker (or a nutcracker), and a mallet; and offer the mustard sauce on the side (recipe below), along with melted butter, and fresh squeezed lemon juice.

MUSTARD SAUCE

YIELD: 1 cup
COOK TIME: 10 minutes

---

1 tablespoon Coleman's dry mustard
1 cup mayonnaise
2 teaspoons Worcestershire sauce

1 teaspoon A-1 steak sauce
1 tablespoon light cream
Salt to taste

Combine the dry mustard, mayonnaise, Worcestershire sauce, A-1 steak sauce, and cream, and add salt to taste. Serve immediately or chill for later use. This sauce is also good on grilled fish or even crab cakes, as an alternative sauce. It's even great with grilled lamb and other meats. It's an excellent all-purpose, creamy, mustard-based sauce.

SAUTÉED GROUPER
WITH PEANUT SAUCE

Pan sautéed fish is best with skin on versus skin off, but I've cooked it both ways. The skin protects the fish from burning and allows the cooking of the fish to be a bit indirect. Always start the sauté with the skin down in the pan. Cook the fillet until the skin is well done and crisp. This takes a little longer, so let it cook beyond when you think it should be done, to avoid sticking to the pan. Be patient. Then flip the fish and cook the flesh carefully until it browns. Then you're either done, for a thin fillet like a trout, or you should finish by turning the fish back onto the skin side and putting the entire pan into a hot oven (400 degrees F) for 5 to 10 minutes. This final roasting completes the cooking for a thicker, denser fillet such as mahi-mahi, grouper, or snapper.

YIELD: 2 servings
COOK TIME: 30 minutes

- 1 cup cooked brown rice
- ½ pepper, green, red, or yellow, or any combination thereof, coarsely chopped
- ½ onion, coarsely chopped
- 1 green onion, white and green parts diced
- 2 ounces (about 6) exotic mushrooms, your choice
- 2 tablespoons grapeseed, peanut or canola oil
- 1 (12-ounce) grouper fillet, preferably skin on
- 2 tablespoons peanut sauce (I use Thai Kitchen brand)
- ½ cup chicken stock

Prepare the brown rice according to package instructions, and set aside.

Preheat the oven to 350 degrees F.

Heat the oil in a large cast-iron skillet over medium-high heat, place the grouper skin-side down and sauté about 5 minutes, turning once, until browned on both sides. Remove the fish from the skillet and set aside while you sauté the vegetables.

Add the peppers, onion, green onion, and mushrooms to the skillet and sauté about 5 minutes, or until they are soft. Lower the heat to medium, add the Thai Kitchen Peanut Sauce and chicken stock, stir, and cook for 15 minutes until it thickens into a gravy. Add the fish back to the skillet.

Serve over brown rice with a Simple Green Salad with light vinaigrette (recipe, page 37).

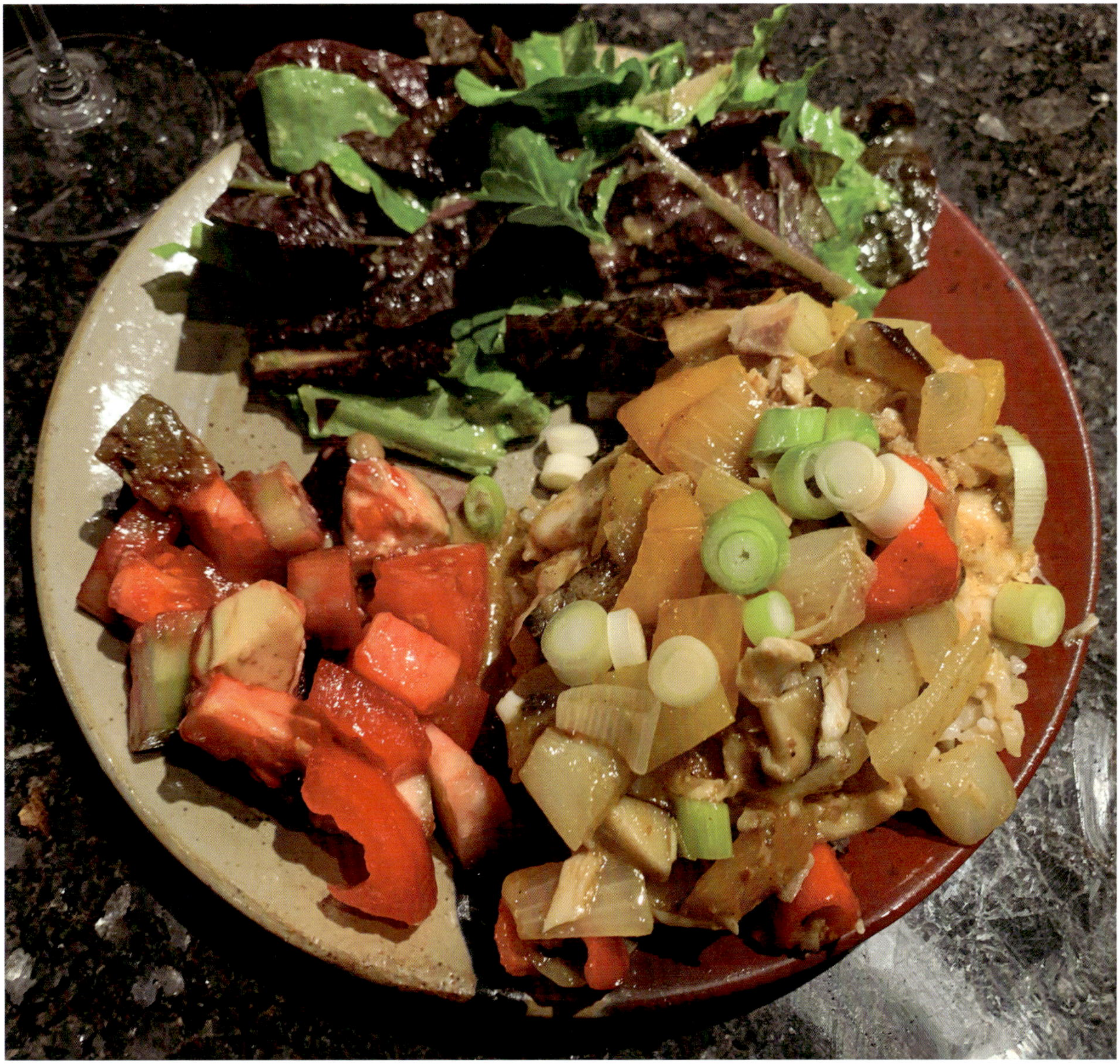

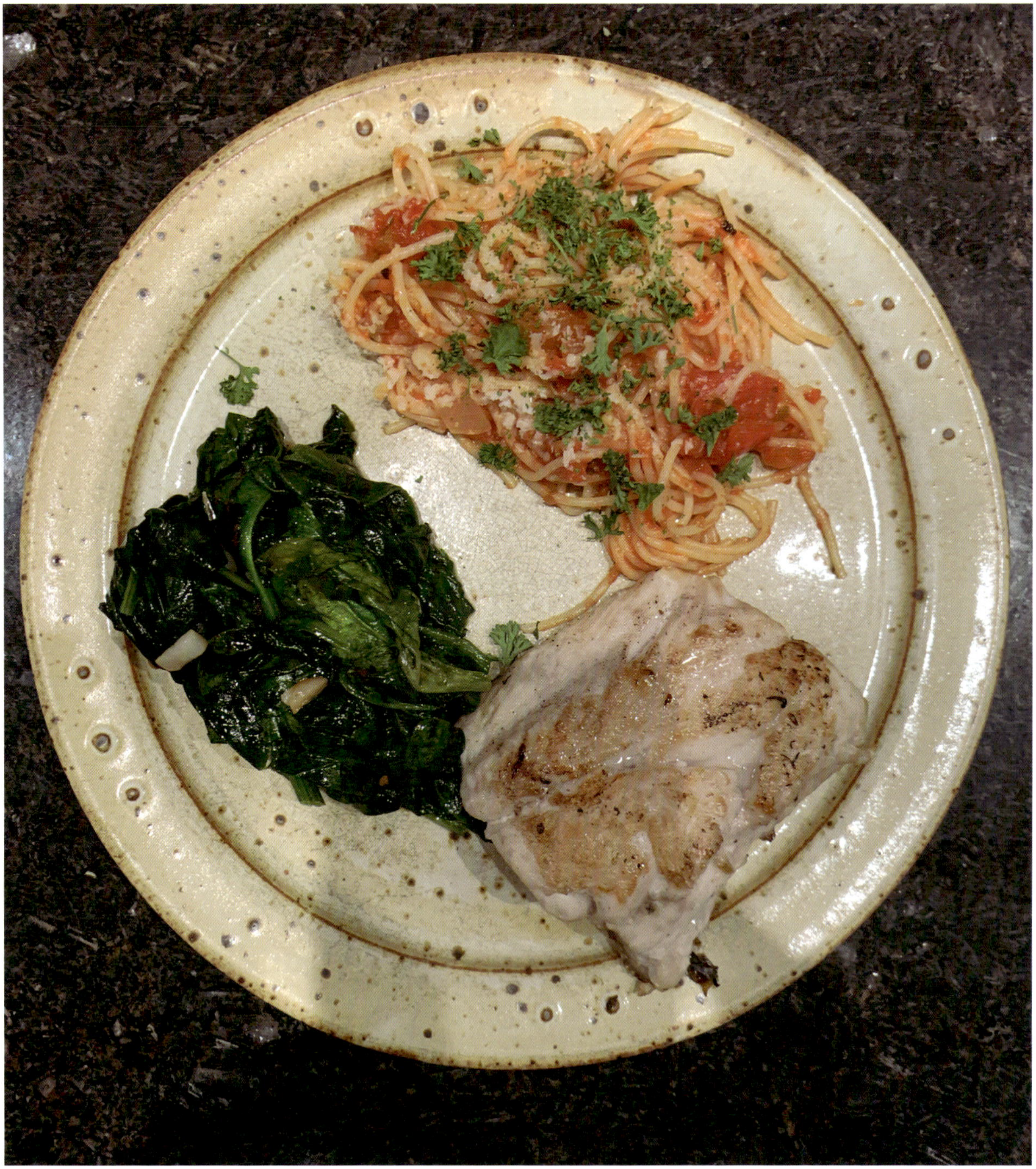

MAHI-MAHI FILLETS
WITH SAUTED SPINACH AND PASTA

YIELD: 2 servings
COOK TIME: 30 to 45 minutes

12 ounces fresh mahi-mahi fillet, skin on
2 tablespoons grapeseed, peanut, or canola oil
Salt

Preheat the oven to 375 degrees F.
  Pat the fillets dry with a paper town and place on a plate. Coat them lightly with oil and salt. You can use an olive oil spray if you'd prefer.
  Sear the fillets in a hot cast iron skillet over medium-high heat, placing them skin-side down and cooking for 5 minutes until brown and crispy; then turn and cook another 5 minutes.
  Place the entire skillet with fish fillets into the preheated oven and roast for 10 minutes, skin-side down.
  Add salt and pepper to taste and serve warm.

PASTA IN RAW TOMATO SAUCE

YIELD: 2 servings
COOK TIME: 30 minutes

8 ounces angel hair pasta
1 tablespoon olive oil
2 whole ripe tomatoes, crushed or finely chopped
2 cloves garlic, diced
½ onion, diced
2 tablespoons shredded Parmesan cheese

Cook the pasta according to package instructions and set aside, saving ½ cup of the pasta water.
  Add the olive oil to a medium pan over medium heat, and sauté the crushed tomato, garlic, and onions for 10 minutes, or until the tomatoes break down and the onions are tender.
  Thin the sauce out with the pasta water and cook 5 to 10 minutes more, or until the liquid is reduced by half. Toss the pasta with the sauce, and top with Parmesan cheese.

GRILLED SALMON

I like to serve this with grilled cauliflower and a simple green salad. It's really great with a lightly brushed glaze of a teriyaki sauce or hoisin sauce, and a light dusting of dried dill. Over the years, I've used Yashita sauce, which they used to sell in big containers at Costco, but lately it's been missing. I have found it at Kroger in recent days.

YIELD: 2 servings
COOK TIME: 30 minutes

¼ cup teriyaki sauce
2 tablespoons extra-virgin olive oil
2 (6 to 8-ounce) salmon fillets, skin on

Salt and pepper to taste
1 tablespoon dried dill

Whisk together the teriyaki sauce and extra-virgin olive oil in a small bowl.

Coat the salmon with the teriyaki mixture, and sprinkle with salt, pepper, and dried dill.

Preheat a Big Green Egg, or other grill, to 350 degrees F.

Grill the salmon skin-side down for 15 minutes; then turn and grill the flesh side for 5 minutes, or until grill marks appear.

Serve with grilled cauliflower and a Simple Green Salad with Vinaigrette (recipe, page 37).

65

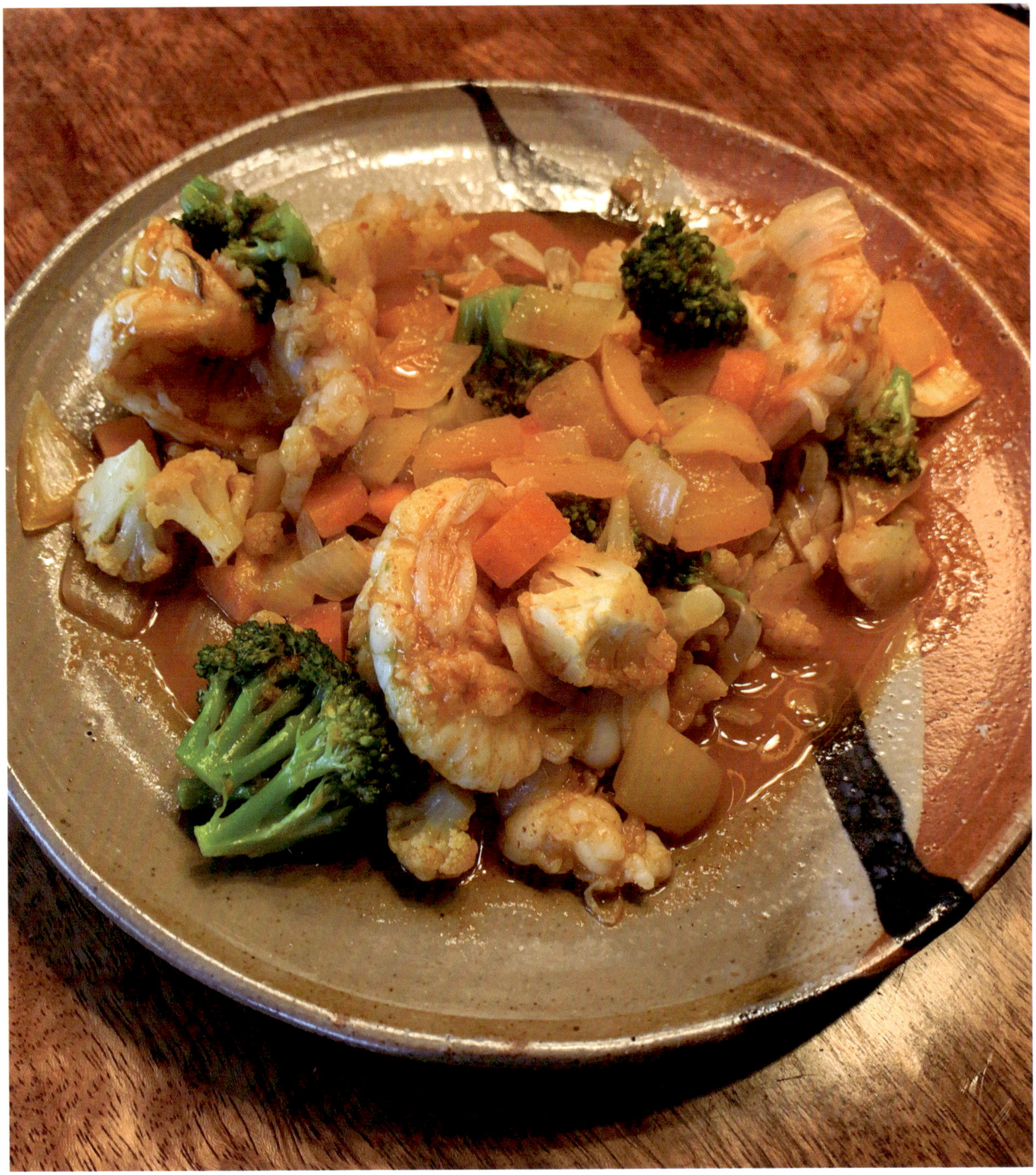

THAI CHILI SHRIMP

YIELD: 4 to 6 servings
COOK TIME: 20 to 30 minutes

---

1 cup cooked brown rice
2 tablespoons grapeseed, canola, or peanut oil
½ onion, finely chopped
1 carrot, coarsely chopped
½ pepper, coarsely chopped (red, green, and/or yellow)
1 clove garlic, minced
1 tablespoon minced ginger
¼ cauliflower, cut into bite-sized pieces
¼ broccoli, cut into bite-sized pieces
1 pound fresh shrimp, peeled
¼ cup light coconut milk
2 tablespoons Thai chili sauce (I like Thai Kitchen brand)

Cook the brown rice according to package directions and set aside.

In a large pan or wok, heat the oil over medium heat and sauté the onion, carrot, peppers, garlic, and ginger for 2 minutes. Once they turn translucent, but are not brown, add the cauliflower, broccoli, and shrimp. Cook 2 more minutes, or until the shrimp turns pink.

Remove from the heat and stir in the coconut milk and Thai Chili sauce.

Return the pan to medium-low heat and simmer about 5 minutes to blend the flavors and warm the milk.

Serve immediately over the brown rice.

SHRIMP FAJITA
WITH CONDIMENTS

YIELD: 2 to 4 servings
COOK TIME: 30 minutes

---

1 cup cooked brown rice
1 cup (8 ounces) guacamole (recipe, page 23)
1 (8-ounce) can black beans, drained and rinsed
½ onion, thinly sliced
2 ounces shiitake mushrooms, thinly sliced

½ pepper (red, green and/or yellow), thinly sliced
2 tablespoons grapeseed, canola, or peanut oil
1 pound shrimp, heads removed and shelled
1 head Romaine lettuce, chopped

Cook the brown rice according to package directions and set aside.

Make the guacamole and set aside.

Puree the black beans using an immersion blender and set aside.

Add the oil to a cast iron skillet over medium heat and sauté the onion, mushrooms, and peppers for 3 minutes, or until they are soft and translucent.

Add the shrimp and continue cooking until pink, about 3 minutes.

Serve over rice with chopped Romaine, black beans, and guacamole on the side.

You can also serve with warm tortillas, if you would like a wrap.

The shrimp and scallops are on the left, and the assembled dish with pasta and Parmesan cheese is on the right. The pecans are roasted, buttered, and spiced.

GRILLED SHRIMP & SCALLOPS
WITH PASTA

YIELD: 2 to 4 servings
COOK TIME: 30 minutes, plus marinating time

---

1 cup cooked angel hair pasta
¼ cup grapeseed, canola, or peanut oil, plus 2 tablespoons, divided
1 tablespoon kosher salt
4 cloves garlic, minced, divided
½ pound shrimp, peeled and deveined
½ pound scallops
½ onion, chopped
1 pepper (red, green, and/or yellow), coarsely chopped
¼ cup coarsely chopped fresh parsley
2 tablespoons grated Parmesan cheese, optional

Cook the pasta according to package directions and set aside.

Combine ¼ cup oil, the salt, and 2 cloves minced garlic in a large bowl.

Add the shrimp and scallops to mixture and marinate, refrigerated, for 30 minutes to 1 hour.

On a gas, propane, or wood burning grill, cook the shrimp and scallops for about 10 minutes, or until pink. Do not overcook the fish. Set aside and keep warm, covered lightly on a plate or in a medium bowl.

In a large sauté pan at medium-high heat, add 2 tablespoons oil and sauté the onions, 2 cloves garlic, and the peppers. When vegetables are translucent, reduce the heat to medium and add the cooked pasta. Top the pasta and vegetables with the grilled shrimp and scallops and sprinkle with fresh parsley and, optionally, Parmesan cheese. Some people don't like cheese with shellfish or fish, but I like the flavor enhancement it adds to the dish. Serve immediately.

Hot Tip:
This is one of Critic Robin's favorite dishes!

GRILLED STRIPED BASS

I love to cook whole fish on my Big Green Egg (BGE), which is both a grill and a smoker that uses natural wood/coal, never any coal with any chemicals. I also cook fish fillets on my BGE. I set my temperature at 350 degrees, which only takes about 15 minutes to do with a BGE, and I cook most whole fish in 20-30 minutes, till well grilled and tender. In addition to grilling, the BGE offers a wood smoke flavor to the flesh of the fish. My favorite whole fish are stripped bass and bronzini, which is a type of Mediterranean bass, both of which are readily available at a good fish market or grocery store with a fresh fish selection.

YIELD: 2 to 4 servings
COOK TIME: 30 minutes

---

2 (1 pound) whole striped bass, scales and guts removed
Canola oil Spray
1 tablespoon extra-virgin olive oil
1 tablespoon salt

1 tablespoon oregano, dried or fresh
1 tablespoon rosemary, dried or fresh
1 teaspoon pepper
2 tablespoons extra-virgin olive oil
1 tablespoon parsley, dried or fresh

Preheat the grill to 350 degrees F.

Place the fish on a cookie sheet, and spray both sides and the insides with oil.

Score both sides of the fish skin on a bias every 2 to 3 inches; try not to cut too far into the flesh.

In a small bowl, combine the oil, salt, oregano, rosemary, and pepper, and rub onto both sides of the fish and in the cavity.

Grill for 20 minutes; then drizzle extra-virgin olive oil and garnish with parsley.

To serve, use a knife and fork to pull the meat off the bone, starting in the middle of the spine and pulling to the sides. Then remove the head and the bone from the bottom half, picking out any small bones that are missed. Serve each person half the fillet, drizzle with olive oil and sprinkle with parsley.

I like to serve this with Roasted Potatoes (recipe, page 129) and a Simple Green Salad with vinaigrette (recipe, page 37).

Meat

GRILLED T-BONE

RACK OF LAMB

ROASTED LEG OF LAMB

GRILLED LAMB CHOPS

BONE-IN-FILET

STEAK FAJITAS

BISON LASAGNA

SPATCHCOCKED CHICKEN

SPINALIS STEAK

CHICKEN KEBAB
WITH VEGETABLE FRIED RICE

CHICKEN & SHRIMP KEBAB

CHICKEN STIR FRY

CHICKEN PAD THAI

CORNISH HEN

ROASTED QUAIL

73

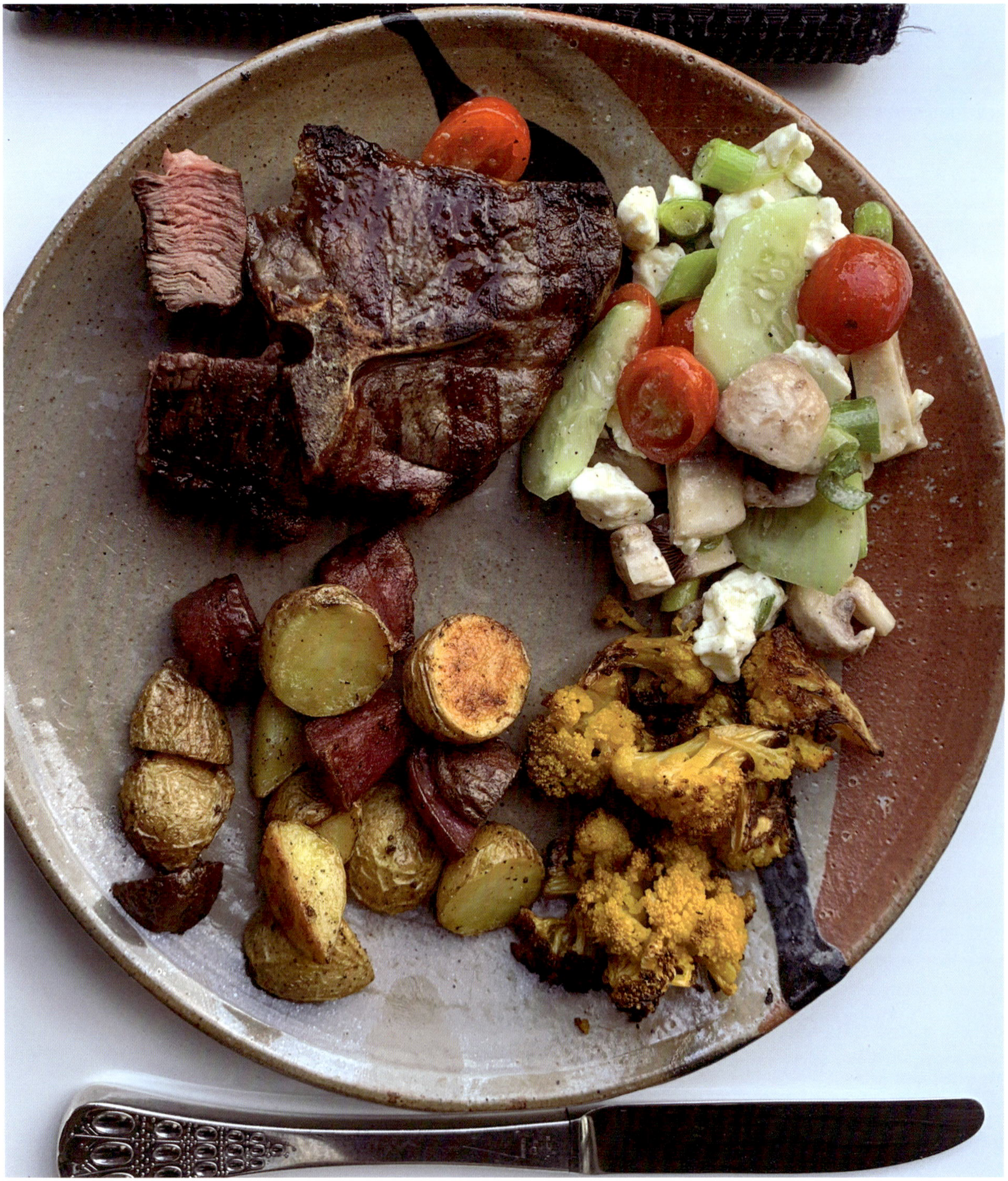

GRILLED T-BONE

This steak is 1/2 filet and 1/2 rib-eye. It's a smaller version of a Porterhouse. I like to serve it with Roasted Potatoes (recipe, page 129), Roasted cauliflower (recipe, page 129), and Cucumber, Tomato, and Feta Salad (recipe, page 36) on the side.

YIELD: 2 to 4 servings
COOK TIME: 15 minutes, plus 5 to 10 minutes to sit at room temperature

---

1 pound T-bone steak, preferably 1-inch thick
1 tablespoon kosher salt

Preheat a gas, propane, or wood-burning grill to a high heat.
Bring the steak to room temperature for at least 30 minutes before cooking.
When you are ready to grill, sprinkle the steak with salt on both sides.
Grill to your desired finish, depending on thickness. For this steak, that is around 5 minutes for rare and up to 10 minutes for well done. Turn once halfway through cooking, and rotate the meat 180 degrees once on each side to give it grill marks.
When done, let it sit for 5 to 10 minutes, then slice it on a bias.

> **Hot Tip:** Keep in mind that all meats need to rest for awhile after cooking to allow them to stop cooking. I've been told that meats should rest for as long as it cooked. So, a chicken that might take 45 minutes could easily rest for 45 minutes before serving—but at least for 10 to 15 minutes.

RACK OF LAMB

A rack is from the center of the lamb ribs and is otherwise known as rib chops. A rack usually weighs about 1½ pounds and generally has 8 chops. It can be cooked pre-cut into chops or double chops, or it can be cooked intact. It is more expensive than a loin chop, which is a fine alternative. I like to serve this with Grilled Eggplant or Eggplant Parmesan (recipe, page 133); Steamed Artichokes (recipe, page 134); a baked potato stuffed with sour cream, butter and Parmesan cheese (recipe, page 128); and Mushroom Risotto (recipe, page 135). Robin says this meal is another favorite of hers.

YIELD: 4 servings, 2 chops per person
COOK TIME: 30 minutes for marinating, 10 minutes to cook

---

1 (1½ pound) rack of lamb, usually 8 chops
2 tablespoons Dijon mustard
¼ cup breadcrumbs, or panko
1 teaspoon salt
1 teaspoon pepper

1 to 2 tablespoons fresh chopped rosemary, or
  1 tablespoon dry rosemary
¼ cup fresh chopped parsley
¼ cup mint jelly (your choice brand)

Preheat the oven to 400 degrees F.

In a large cast iron skillet on high heat, braise the rack of lamb chops about 5 minutes, or until browned on both sides. Let the lamb rest at room temperature for 5 to 10 minutes.

In a medium bowl, combine the mustard, breadcrumbs, salt, pepper and rosemary thoroughly. Coat the entire rack of lamb with the mixture.

Place the rack of lamb in a shallow pan and bake for 15 minutes, then reduce heat to 350 degrees F. and continue cooking for 10 minutes. This will produce a medium finish. (The photo on the right is more of a medium rare, and I cooked it for a total of 15 to 20 minutes in the oven.) Transfer the cooked lamb to a plate and let it sit for 15 minutes; then carve into 8 individual chops.

Garnish with parsley before serving, and use mint jelly as a side.

There's nothing better than a spicy, full-bodied wine with lamb chops. I prefer Chateauneuf du Pape, which is a predominantly grenache grape, although they are allowed to use thirteen different grape varieties. Other wine from the northern Rhone River region of France can include more syrah-forward wines, such as Hermitage. CDNP wines are from the southern Rhone area. Another great alternative would be an American Zinfandel wine.

ROASTED LEG OF LAMB

YIELD: 6 to 8 servings
COOK TIME: 20 to 30 minutes

---

1 (2 to 2½-pound) butterflied leg of lamb
¼ cup honey
2 tablespoons soy sauce

1 tablespoon pepper
2 tablespoons rosemary

Flatten out the butterflied leg (this often comes from the butcher rolled and tied with string).
 Mix all remaining ingredients together, and coat the lamb on all sides. Place in a large baking pan, and let the lamb marinate for 1 hour or more.
 Preheat a Big Green Egg, or propane, gas, or wood-burning grill to 350 degrees F.
 Grill the lamb for 20 to 30 minutes, depending upon your desired doneness.
 Let the lamb sit at room temperature for 10 to 20 minutes before slicing into 1- to 2-inch slices.
 Serve immediately, warm.

GRILLED LAMB CHOPS

Served here with Vegetable Fried Rice (recipe, page 126).

YIELD: 4 servings, 2 chops per person
COOK TIME: 30 minutes to marinate, 10 minutes to cook

---

1 cup extra-virgin olive oil
½ cup red wine vinegar
1 teaspoon salt
1 teaspoon pepper

2 to 4 tablespoons fresh rosemary, or
   2 tablespoons dried rosemary
1 rack of lamb, cut into 8 chops, each about
   1-inch thick; or into 4 double chops

In a large ziplock bag, combine the oil, vinegar, salt, pepper, and rosemary. Add the lamb chops, rub the marinate over the chops thoroughly, refrigerate, and marinate for at least 30 minutes, or all day (the longer, the tastier).

Grill on a very hot grill for 5 to 10 minutes, flipping midway through cooking, for a medium-rare finish, depending on the thickness of meat.

Let the chops rest at room temperature for 10 minutes before serving.

BONE-IN-FILET

A bone-in filet is a filet mignon that is still attached to its bone. It's generally sold without the bone as a prime filet or a petit filet, in 6 to 8-ounce cuts, or it can be bought as a complete tenderloin in 4-pound cuts from the back ribcage of a cow. In the latter case, one would roast the steak and cut it after cooking it or cut it into individual steaks of 6 ounces each and then cook it. In this case, this is a filet mignon tenderloin steak with bone still attached. After cooking, it can be served intact, although it's a pretty big serving, or cut off the bone and then sliced. I like to serve my meats sliced, making it easier to handle at the table. I also find that when pre-sliced, a smaller portion (say 4 to 6 ounces) can be equally filling as a larger portion (8 ounces).

YIELD: 2 servings
COOK TIME: 10 minutes, or more

---

1 (12 to 16-ounce) filet with bone-in, about 1½ to 2-inches thick

1 tablespoon salt

2 tablespoons extra-virgin olive oil

Place the filet on plate and bring to room temperature.

Sprinkle with salt and drizzle with extra-virgin olive oil. Let sit for 30 to 60 minutes at room temperature.

Grill at high temperature to your desired doneness. Medium-rare takes about 10 minutes.

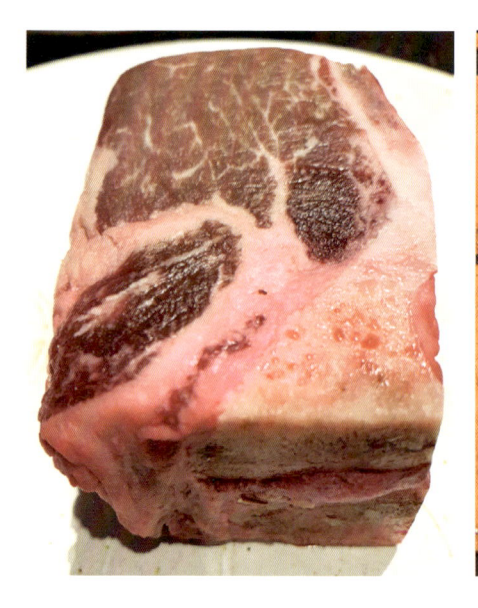

Robin says:
"Whatever you do, don't overcook it. I like it raw!"

81

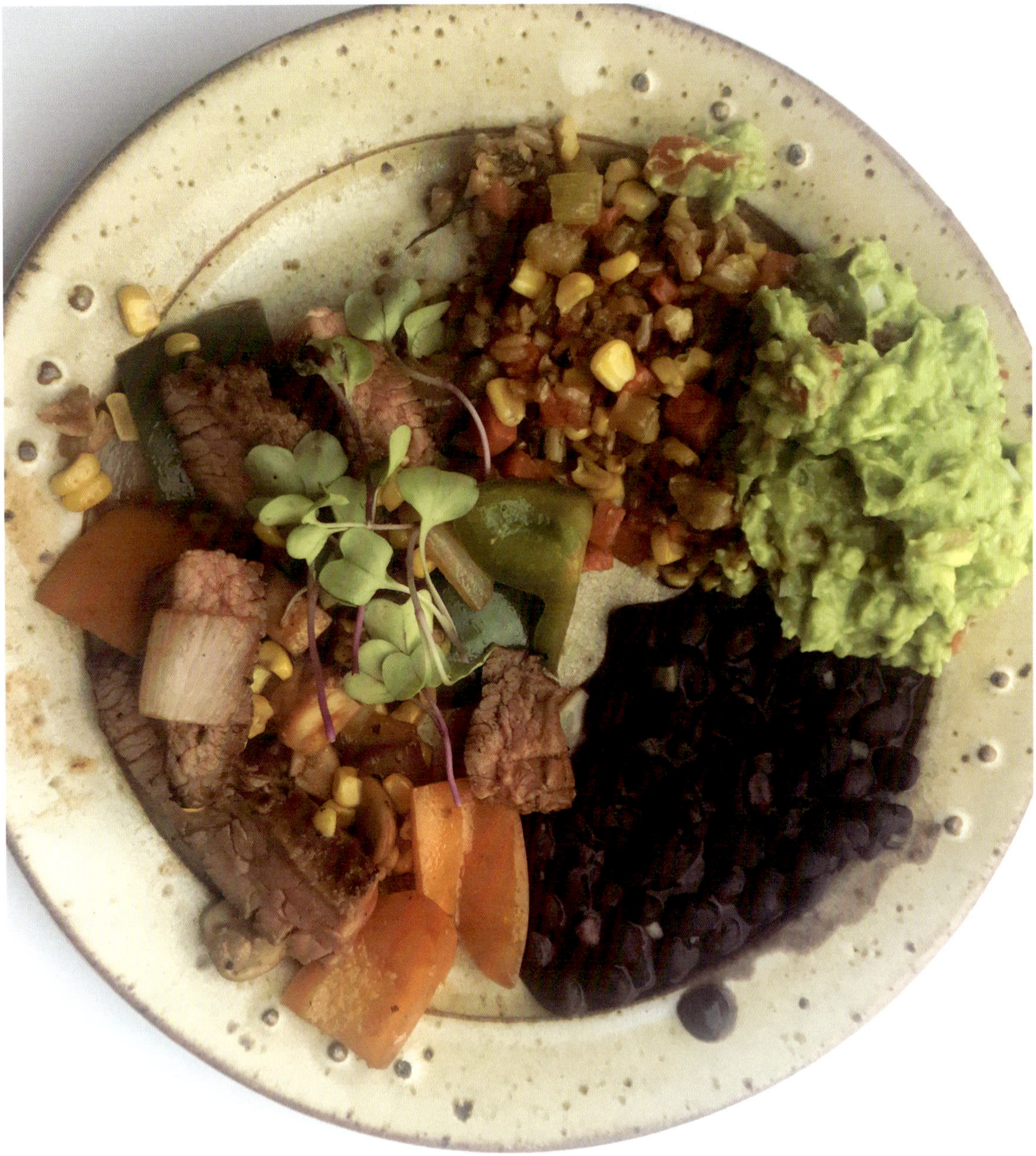

STEAK FAJITAS

Fajitas are just a variation on the theme of a stir fry. One is traditionally Mexican, while the other is traditionally Asian. I find that there are many variations on a theme and that most nationalities have similar dishes, just named differently, but with similar ingredients. The main difference may be the way the dish is served (e.g., fajitas with tortillas, stir fry with rice) and the garnish, or herbs.

YIELD: 4 servings
COOK TIME: 20 minutes

1 (16-ounce) flank or skirt steak, or hangar, or flatiron	1 tablespoon grapeseed, canola, or peanut oil
Grapeseed, canola, or peanut oil spray	1 onion, coarsely sliced
Salt	1 pepper, (red, green, and/or yellow), cut into 1-inch pieces

Rinse the steak and dry it; bring it to room temperature, and then spray overall with oil and sprinkle lightly with salt.

Heat a gas, propane, or wood-burning grill to high, and grill the steak until rare, no more than 5 minutes. you'd really like the steak to be rare at this point, since you will be combining it with the sauteed vegetables and cooking it a little more. Set aside.

In a cast iron skillet on medium heat, add the oil and sauté the sliced onion and peppers for 3 minutes, or until soft. Once soft and translucent, add the steak and cook only to warm; don't overcook.

When ready to serve, cut into ½-inch slices on the bias. Garnish with fresh cilantro and serve hot.

MAKING THE CUT
These cuts have traditionallly been a butcher's cheap, throwaway cuts. They are all great to coook, though!

Skirt— a cow's diaphragm muscle, thin, fibrous, separates chest from abdomen. The least tender of the three others, in need of marinade.

Flank— on the belly close to hind legs, super lean. Also takes marinade. Best choice for fajita, bibimbap and, of course, Philly cheese steak (I'm from Philly). Also known as "London broil"

Hanger— hangs between tenderloin and the rib. From deep inside the loin making it relatively tender. Called "the hanging tender." A good steak, often used in steak frites, the famous French bistro dish.

Flatiron— off shoulder blade, petit tender or top blade steak.

> **Hot Tip:**
> I recently discovered lasagna noodles that don't need precooking; you can simply assemble the lasagna with the uncooked noodles and cook it. I still prefer the variety that needs cooking, but it requires one more step in preparation. It's your call.

BISON LASAGNA

I like to serve this with a Grilled Caesar Salad (recipe, page 35).

YIELD: 4 to 6 servings
COOK TIME: 45 minutes

---

3 lasagna noodles
2 tablespoons grapeseed, canola or peanut oil
½ onion, chopped
2 cloves garlic, minced
½ pepper (red, green, and/or yellow)
1 pound ground bison
1 (16-ounce) can whole peeled tomatoes, preferably Marzano

2 tablespoons fresh oregano, if possible
⅛ teaspoon red pepper flakes
Salt and pepper to taste
½ cup shredded mozzarella cheese
½ cup Parmesan cheese
2 tablespoons coarsely chopped parsley

Preheat the oven to 350 degrees F.

Cook the lasagna noodles according to package directions, and set aside.

Add the oil to a large sauté pan on medium heat, sauté onions, garlic, and peppers until translucent, about 5 minutes.

Add the ground bison to the vegetable mixture and cook until brown, about 10 minutes.

Add the tomatoes and spices and stir until everything is well blended. Remove from the heat.

In a 5 x 9-inch pan, spread a thin layer of sauce. Add a layer of noodles, then a layer of sauce, and sprinkle with mozzarella cheese. Repeat the above with three layers of noodles and ending with a final layer of mozzarella cheese.

Bake in the middle of the oven for 30 minutes until all the cheese is melted. If you want to brown the top, broil it for 2 to 3 minutes, being careful not to burn the cheese.

Garnish with parsley and grated Parmesan cheese and serve.

SPATCHCOCKED CHICKEN

A spatchcocked chicken is simply a whole chicken that is split in half down the spine side of the bird (the breast side is left intact), and then flattened. It cooks much quicker than a whole roasted chicken, with great results, in 30 minutes. There is more skin contact with the grill, providing a crispier skin. I like to cook it on a Big Green Egg for a barbecue flavor. Most grocery stores carry pre-spatchcocked chickens; some are even pre-marinated, but it's quite easy to spatchcock a chicken yourself, using either a large sharp chef's knife or a good pair of poultry scissors.

YIELD: 4 servings
COOK TIME: 1 hour

1 whole chicken, spatchcocked
2 tablespoons oil
2 tablespoons butter
2 tablespoons dried oregano
1 tablespoon paprika
1 tablespoon salt
1 tablespoon pepper

Preheat a Big Green Egg to 350 degrees F.

To spatchcock a whole chicken, remove the backbone. Push down on the breastbone to flatten it out. You can also buy a chicken that has already been spatchcocked.

Cover the skin with the oil, and put butter underneath skin at the breasts and legs/thighs.

Sprinkle the oregano, paprika, salt, and pepper over all the bird.

Cook on a Big Green Egg for 45 minutes, or until the meat is falling-off-the-bone tender.

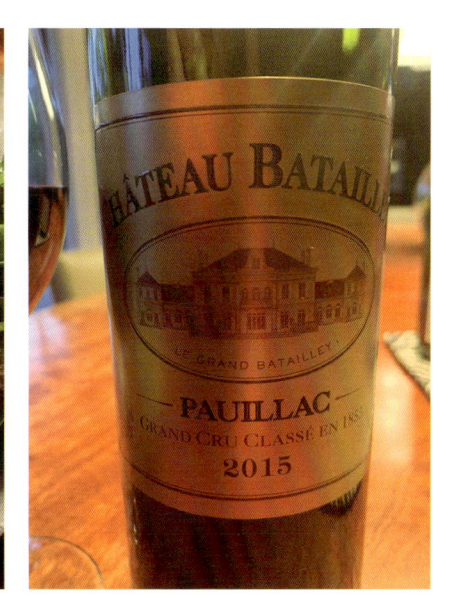

SPINALIS STEAK

Spinalis is also known as the "top cap" of the ribeye; it is generally a thin cut, 1-inch plus or minus thickness, since it's a cap; but it is highly marbleized, making it taste great. Just about every time I serve it for guests, they say that it's the best steak they've ever had, although it's not the prettiest piece of meat. I tend to slice it before serving so that a small amount can go a long way. Robin and I often split a 6 to 8-ounce filet.

Red meat says "red wine" to me. In fact, it says complex, full bodied, Cabernet Sauvignon, or Bordeaux'. We had this steak with a wonderful French Bordeaux from the area of Paulliac, along the Gironde River. This wine is 85% Cabernet Sauvignon, and it has a strong, velvety, full-bodied taste. It's a great addition to a wonderful spinalis steak.

YIELD: 1 to 2 servings
COOK TIME: 20 minutes

1 (8-ounce) spinalis steak

Cook on a grill at high heat for a quick 4 to 6 minutes, turning regularly. Do not overcook.
  Slice the steak against the grain, into thin, ½-inch thick slices, on the bias.
  Serve with a Baked Potato (recipe, page 128) and a Simple Green Salad (recipe, page 37).

CHICKEN KEBAB

YIELD: 4 servings
COOK TIME: 20 to 30 minutes

---

1 cup cooked veggie fried rice (recipe, page 126)
1 pound chicken, white and/or dark meat, deboned and cut into ½- to 1-inch cubes
½ pineapple, cut into 1-inch cubes
1 pepper (red, green and/or yellow), cut in 1-inch cubes

1 onion, cubed
6 mushrooms
2 tablespoons soy sauce
2 tablespoons grapeseed, canola or peanut oil
1 tablespoon salt
1 tablespoon pepper

Cook the rice, and set aside until it is time to serve; then quickly reheat.
  Preheat a propane, gas, or wood-burning grill to 350 degrees F.
  Soak 4 long wooden kebab sticks in water for 5 to 10 minutes.
  Place the chicken, pineapple, pepper, onion, and mushroom cubes on sticks or metal kebabs, and lay them on a large cookie sheet. Mix the soy sauce, oil, salt, and pepper and sprinkle on the kebabs as a marinade for 30 minutes, or up to 8 hours.
  Grill for 15 minutes, turning every 5 minutes.
  Serve immediately with veggie fried rice.

CHICKEN & SHRIMP KEBAB
ON GREENS

YIELD: 4 servings
COOK TIME: 30 minutes

½ pound chicken, white and/or dark meat, deboned and cut into 1-inch cubes
½ pound fresh shrimp, shelled
2 tablespoons grapeseed, canola or peanut oil
1 onion, diced

2 cloves garlic, minced
4 cups chopped greens (mustard, collards, spinach, or combination thereof)
¼ cup chicken stock, or water

Preheat a propane, gas, or wood-burning grill to 350 degrees F.
  Soak four long wooden kebab sticks in water for 5 to 10 minutes, or use metal kebabs.
  Assemble the kebabs with alternating shrimp and chicken cubes.
  Grill the kebabs for 5 to 10 minutes, turning once halfway through cooking. Transfer to a plate and cover with foil to keep warm.
  Add the oil to a saucepot over medium heat and sauté the onions and garlic until translucent, about 5 minutes. Stir in the chopped greens and cook until tender, about 1 or 2 minutes.
  Add chicken stock or water just to cover bottom of pot, and bring to a constant, slow simmer. If the pan gets dry, add a littler more water. Cook for 15 to 30 minutes, or until well done and tender.
  Drain and use the greens as a bed for the kebabs.

90

CHICKEN STIR FRY

This is one of the most versatile dishes in my repertoire. It can be used with any protein, meat or fish, and it can be used with fresh uncooked protein, or with leftovers. I make it as chicken, beef, shrimp and fish, from time to time. You can even combine proteins like steak and chicken, or surf and turf. If using leftovers, add the protein at the end of the cooking time, just to reheat the leftover protein.

YIELD: 2 to 4 servings
COOK TIME: 20 to 30 minutes

- 1 cup cooked rice, or angel hair pasta
- 2 tablespoons peanut oil
- 1 teaspoon minced ginger
- 2 cloves garlic, diced
- ½ onion, chopped
- 1 carrot, chopped
- 1 stalk celery, chopped
- 1 pepper, (red, green and/or yellow)
- 2 ounces (6) mushrooms, chopped
- 1 pound chicken, boneless breast and/or thigh and leg, deboned and cut into ½-inch cubes
- ¼ cup chicken stock
- 2 tablespoons hoisin sauce
- 1 teaspoon sriracha sauce, or 2 teaspoons fish sauce, if you're making a shrimp or fish stir fry

---

Cook the rice or pasta according to package directions and set aside.

Heat the oil in a large sauté pan, over medium-high heat, and sauté the ginger, garlic, onions, carrots, celery, peppers, and mushrooms for 5 minutes until cooked al dente.

Add the chicken (or other protein), and stir until the chicken is cooked, about 5 minutes.

Add the chicken stock, hoisin, and sriracha sauce, blend well, and cook about 5 minutes.

Serve hot over the reheated rice or pasta.

CHICKEN PAD THAI

Pad Thai is a Thai variation on stir fry, generally using different noodles like glass or rice noodles. Otherwise, it's a very similar dish except for the inclusion of peanuts.

YIELD: 4 servings
COOK TIME: 30 minutes

---

16 ounces noodles (thin whole wheat pasta noodles, or the more traditional glass rice noodles)
2 tablespoons peanut, canola, or grapeseed oil
2 cloves garlic, minced
1 onion, diced
1 pepper (red, green and/or yellow), diced
2 ounces (2 to 3) shiitake mushrooms, diced
2 green onions, white part only (keep green part for garnish), sliced
1 jalapeño, or serrano pepper, minced

1 pound chicken, deboned, white and/or dark meat, skin removed, and cut in ½-inch cubes
1 egg
1 tablespoon fish sauce
1 tablespoon rice vinegar
1 teaspoon sugar
1 teaspoon paprika
1 teaspoon tamarind paste
¼ cup peanuts, chopped
2 tablespoons micro greens, or cilantro
4 lime wedges

Precook the noodles according to package directions, and set aside.

Add the oil to a large sauté pan over medium-high heat, and cook the garlic, onion, pepper, mushrooms, green onions, and jalapeño in oil for 5 minutes, or until tender.

Add the chicken, and continue to cook for 10 minutes until the chicken has browned a bit.

Lower the heat to medium, add the egg, and scramble it well.

Add the fish sauce, rice vinegar, sugar, paprika, and tamarind, and stir until well mixed.

Stir in the cooked noodles, toss to thoroughly blend, and warm.

To serve, garnish with peanuts, scallions or cilantro, and lime wedges.

93

I think of Cornish hen and quail both as winter-type menus. Considering this perspective, I served them with vegetable fried rice and greens. A very hearty combination. This provided for a good combination of vegetables and textures, as well as a carbohydrate to round out the plate and the menu. This dish goes well with a medium bodied wine with some spice, like a grenache or syrah, wines that are traditionally from the Rhone region of France. However, they are making great grenache and syrahs from the Californian central coast, such as Paso Robles. If you prefer a little more lightness in your red wine and less spice, a well-balanced pinot noir goes great as well.

CORNISH HEN

A Cornish hen, also known as Rock Cornish hen, is broiler chicken, never weighing more than 2 pounds.

YIELD: 2 servings
COOK TIME: 45 minutes

---

1 whole Cornish hen
1 to 2 tablespoons butter
2 tablespoons Herbs de Provence (a mixture of rosemary, fennel, savory, thyme, basil, marjoram, lavender, parsley, oregano and tarragon)

1 tablespoon salt
1 teaspoon pepper

Preheat the oven to 400 degrees F.
  Rub the skin with butter, put butter under the skin of the breasts, and rub the herbs all over the bird. Place it in a 9 x 12-inch baking dish and let it sit for 30 minutes at room temperature before cooking. Roast on the middle shelf of the oven for 45 minutes. If you want it more browned, broil for 2 to 3 minutes. Cut in half to serve.

ROASTED QUAIL

YIELD: 2 servings
COOK TIME: 1 hour, 30 minutes

> Growing up in South Carolina, we regularly ate squab, which is a young domestic pigeon, and a close cousin to a Quail.
> —Robin

---

2 whole quails
1 orange
2 tablespoons honey

½ teaspoon cumin
2 cloves garlic, minced
2 tablespoons butter

Preheat the oven to 400 degrees F.
  Split the quails in half and place on a sheet pan.
  In a large bowl, combine the orange, honey, cumin, garlic, and butter to create a marinade. Rub this over the quail and let it sit for 1 hour.
  Cook quail in oven on the sheet pan, basting every 10 minutes, for 20 minutes, or until done. If it is not brown, broil for 2 minutes, making sure not to burn.
  Serve hot.

Eggs, Sandwiches, & Starches

FRITTATA

HOLE-IN-ONE

BOTHAM BURGERS

'70s THROWBACK HEALTH SANDWICH

MINI GRILLED CHEESE

CURED SALMON & BAGEL

SPINALIS CHEESESTEAK TORTILLA

GRILLED BISON TORTILLA

GROUPER SANDWICH ON BRIOCHE BUN
WITH MUSTARD SAUCE

ANDOUILLE & MOZZARELLA CALZONE

PIZZA DOUGH

PIZZA & SALAD

PEPPERONI PIZZA

PIZZA TOMATO SAUCE

ANGEL HAIR PASTA

SPINACH PASTA

PASTA WITH RAW TOMATO SAUCE

WHOLE WHEAT SPAGHETTI
WITH CHICKEN & VEGETABLES

CHICKEN & ANDOUILLE PAELLA

97

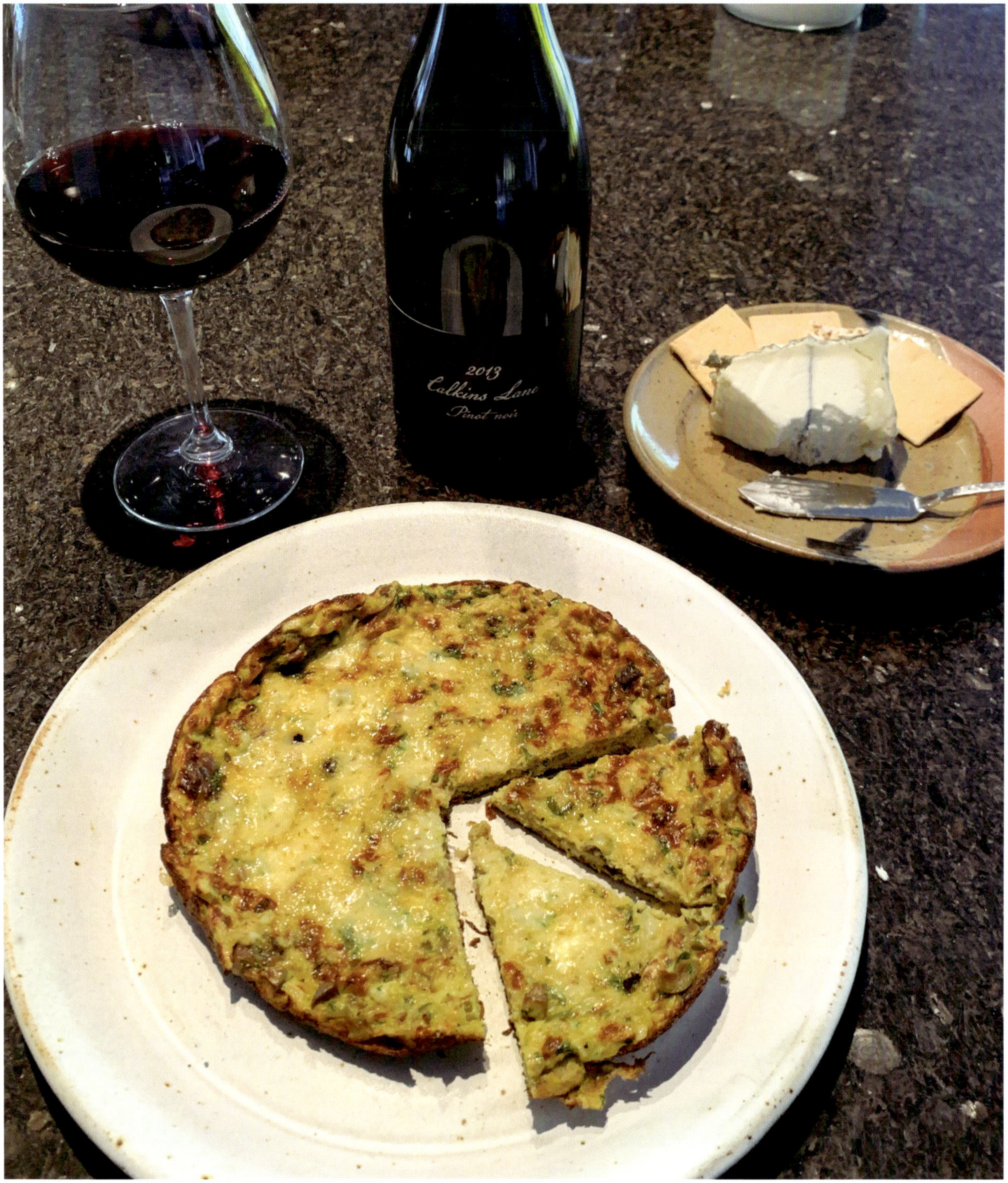
2013
Calkins Lane
Pinot noir

FRITATTA

Frittata is an Italian egg dish that's served at any meal during the day. Although it's mostly thought of as a breakfast dish, it works well at any time of day. The Spanish serve it as an appetizer for dinner or as a snack. It's called a Tortilla Espanola in Spain. It doesn't have to be served hot, but works well at room temperature, and it can have many different kinds of fillings. At this meal, we served it with a medium-bodied pinot noir from Adelsheim Vineyard in Oregon. It works just as well with a full-bodied white wine.

YIELD: 2 servings
COOK TIME: 20 to 30 minutes

---

2 tablespoons butter
4 eggs
2 leeks, whites only, thinly sliced

2 ounces andouille sausage, diced
4 to 6 olives, sliced
2 ounces grated gruyere cheese

Preheat the oven to broil.

Melt the butter in a medium sauté pan over medium heat.

While the butter is melting, whisk the eggs with 1 tablespoon of water then pour into the pan. Cook the eggs for 2 to 3 minutes, like an omelet. With a spatula, lift the edges of the cooked egg to allow the remaining liquid egg to spread over the entire pan evenly.

When the egg is cooked through, add the leeks, sausage, and olives evenly on top, and sprinkle with gruyere cheese. Place the entire pan under a broiler, and broil for 2 to 3 minutes until brown. Do not burn.

Cut in half and serve immediately with a salad.

HOLE-IN-ONE

This may have been the first thing I ever learned to cook, in college. It always raises eyebrows, and everyone loves it. In this case I've served it with mixed melons (honeydew & cantaloupe) and turkey bacon.

YIELD: 1 serving
COOK TIME: 15 minutes

---

1 tablespoon butter
1 slice multi-grain bread
1 egg
Salt and pepper to taste

2 to 3 slices turkey bacon
½ cup seasonal fresh fruit, cut in 1 to 2-inch cubes

Heat a griddle or cast-iron skillet to medium heat.

Butter both sides of the bread lightly and place the bread on the griddle to brown for 1 or 2 minutes, then turn and brown the other side.

Cut a hole in the center of the bread using a a jigger, shot glass, pastry form, or a small can (like one for tomato paste). Place the cut-out center off to the side of the griddle once it's cooked.

Break the egg carefully and let it roll into the middle of the bread. Sprinkle with salt and pepper to taste. I usually flip the egg and bread after about 2-3 minutes to fry both sides of the hole-in-one. of course, the timing depends on whether you like you egg easy or well done.

Serve with fresh fruit and turkey bacon on the side.

> Hot Tip:
> This can be cooked "up" or over easy. It's your choice whether you want to look at an undercooked egg yolk or not.

BOTHAM BURGERS

Named after Ian Botham, one of the most well acclaimed English Cricket players, and made famous by Jamie Oliver. This dish is thanks to our friends, Saa and Ka from South Africa, who ate this cricket-shaped hamburger as kids growing up in JoBurg.

YIELD: 4 servings
COOK TIME: 20 minutes

---

1 tablespoon olive oil
½ red onion, diced
1 carrot, diced
4 ounces (½ cup) panko
16 ounces ground beef
1 tablespoon chopped parsley
1 tablespoon Dijon mustard
1 tablespoon chopped pickle
Salt and pepper to taste
2 ounces cheddar cheese, sliced
4 brioche buns
2 lettuce leaves, cut in half
1 tomato, sliced

Add the olive oil to a large sauté pan on medium heat, and sauté the onions and carrots for 5 minutes until they are translucent.

In a large bowl, combine the sautéed vegetables with the panko, ground beef, and parsley.

Use your hands to form into 4 patties (cricket ball size—hence the name Botham, a famous cricket player).

Place on a hot griddle or skillet, and cook at high heat for 2 to 3 minutes per side until done, pressing down on the patties with a spatula as they cook. Do not overcook. Salt and pepper to taste.

Place the cheese on top of each burger on the griddle just until it melts.

Remove from the heat, and set aside for 5 minutes.

Reduce the griddle heat to medium, and warm opened buns for 2 minutes.

Assemble the burgers with lettuce and tomato, and serve hot.

70s THROWBACK HEALTH SANDWICH

In my early days of cooking, health food was very in, and this sandwich was the most popular made with avocado, whole grain bread, some sort of semi-soft cheese (in this case cheddar or compté), lettuce and tomato. It was/is the health food equivalent to a BLT. It goes well with a small fruit salad, much better than chips. I like watermelon, strawberries, berries, peaches, or whatever is available and most fresh. It really depends on what's happening in at the market. All my cooking depends on what looks best at the market. I go to the market often, and I go to different ones all the time.

YIELD: 4 servings
COOK TIME: 10 minutes

---

4 slices whole grain bread with seeds
1 avocado, smashed
1 teaspoon salt
2 ounces cheese (cheddar or compte), sliced

1 tomato, sliced
2 lettuce leaves, cut in half, or 2 ounces sprouts
1 cup diced fresh fruit

Toast or brown the bread on a griddle, and assemble your sandwiches.

This is great served with a small bowl of diced fresh fruit on the side.

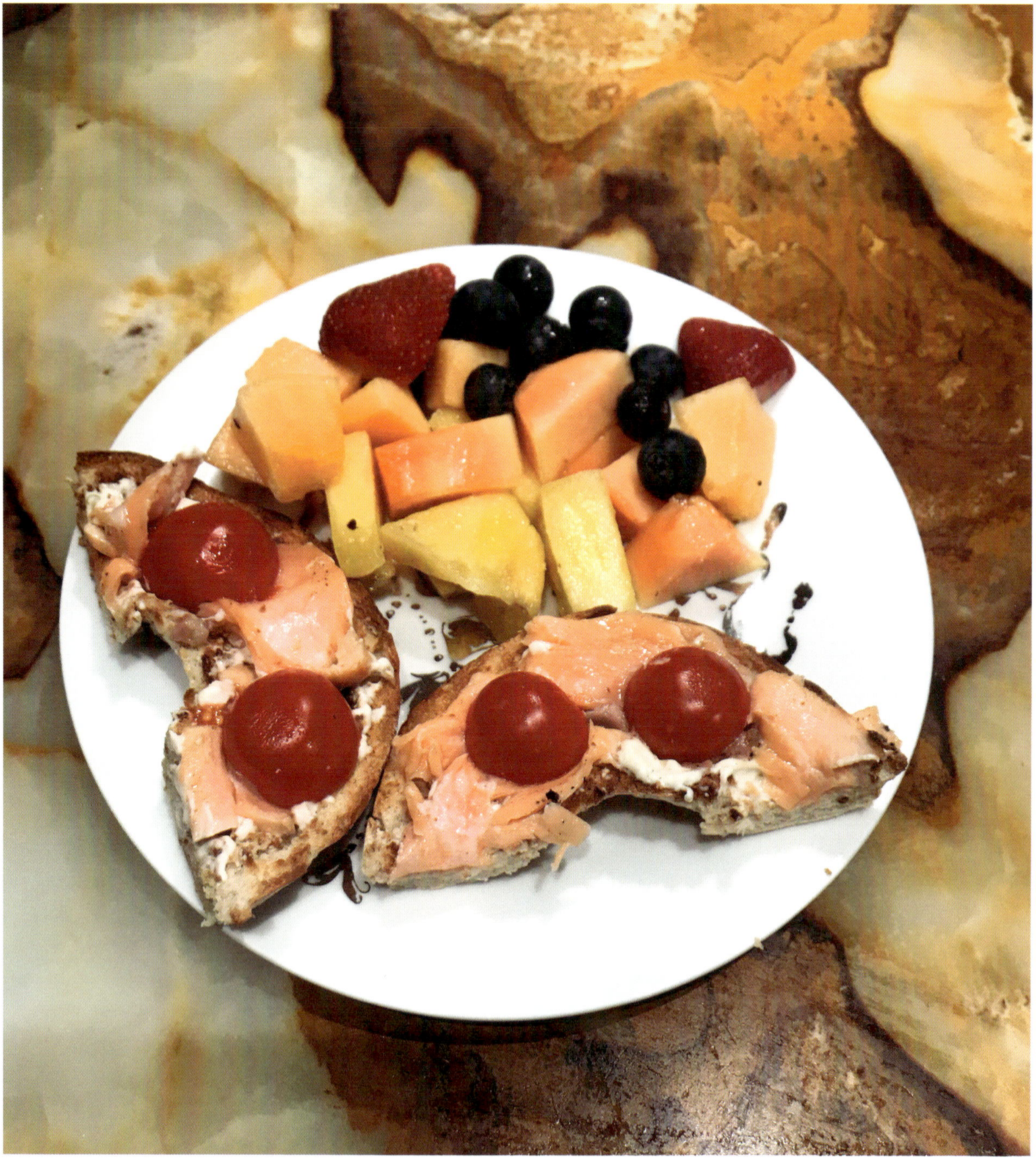

CURED SALMON & BAGEL

Robin likes a toasted, scooped bagel where I cut out the inside of the bread, leaving a shell to toast. It makes for a crispier, less carbohydrate bread, and it allows you to fill in where the bread was so the sandwich doesn't fall apart as much.

YIELD: 2 open-face or 1 traditional sandwich
COOK TIME: 15 minutes

---

1 bagel
2 tablespoons cream cheese
2 to 4 ounces cured salmon (recipe, page 31)

1 tomato, sliced
¼ head lettuce, leaves torn (optional)

Toast the bagel, and spread with cream cheese on both halves.
 Place the salmon on the cream cheese, and top with tomatoes and lettuce leaves.
 Serve as an open-face or traditional sandwich.

MINI GRILLED CHEESE SANDWICH

YIELD: 1 serving
COOK TIME: 15 minutes

---

2 bread slices
2 ounces your choice cheese (I like gruyere or cheddar)
1 tablespoon butter, or oil spray

Assemble a sandwich with cheese.
 Spray a griddle or medium pan with oil, or use melted butter.
 Cook the sandwich in the pan over medium heat for 5 minutes on each side until browned.
 Cut into four pieces and serve hot.

SPINALIS CHEESESTEAK TORTILLA

This is the Mexican version of my favorite Philly cheesesteak with fried onions. It works great with leftover steak, or you can use uncooked meat as a starter; however, it is a bit of waste to use an uncooked, raw steak.

YIELD: 2 tortillas
COOK TIME: 15 minutes

2 tablespoons olive oil
4 to 6 ounces spinalis, sliced
¼ onion, sliced
¼ pepper, (red, green, and/or yellow), sliced
2 ounces (about 4) mushrooms, preferably shiitake, but white button works fine
2 tablespoons grapeseed, canola, or peanut oil
2 ounces mozzarella cheese
2 (8-inch) tortillas

Add the oil to a griddle or a large skillet over medium heat, and sauté the slices of spinalis, onion, peppers, and mushrooms for 5 minutes until tender.

Stir to combine, cover with the cheese, and cook long enough to melt the cheese.

Warm the tortillas in a skillet over medium heat, or wrap the tortillas in foil, and warm them on low-heat (250 degrees F) in the oven for 5 minutes.

Scoop out the cheesesteak with a spatula, place in center of each tortilla, and roll the tortillas up.

Serve hot.

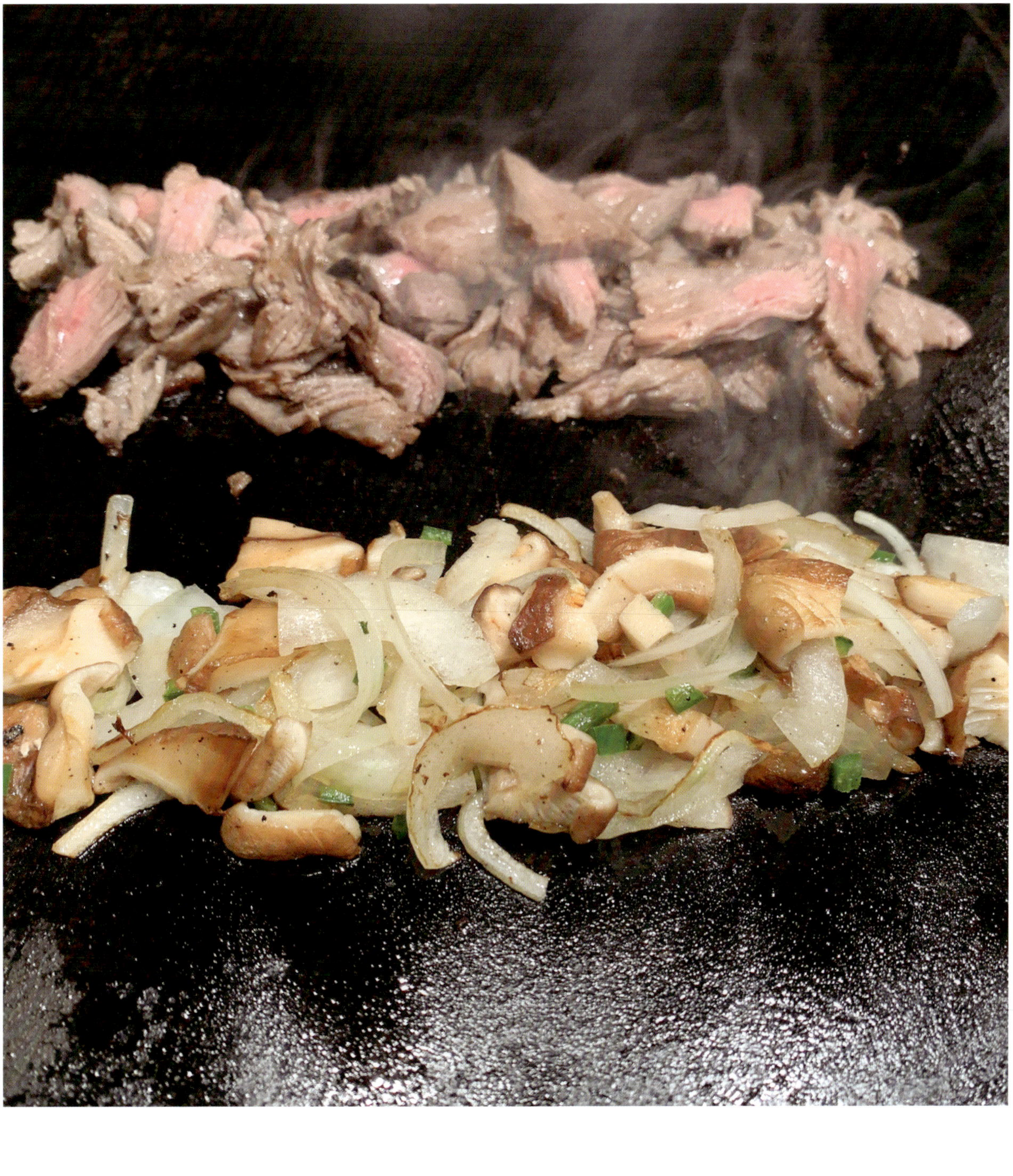

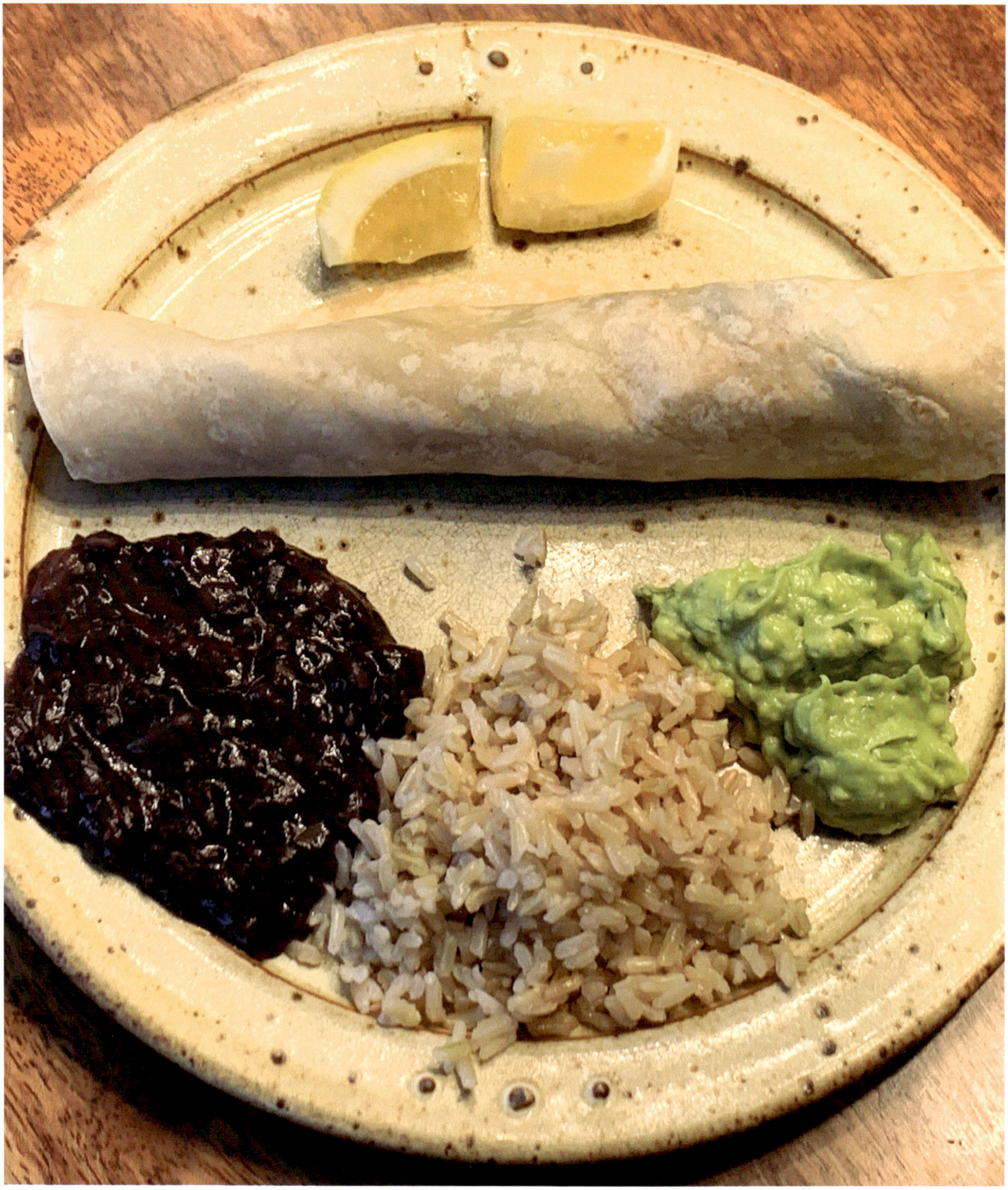

GRILLED BISON TORTILLA

We've started to grow fond of Bison, as an alternative to beef. It's generally a thin(ner) steak than a comparable beef cut without much fat, so you have to be careful not to overcook it and dry it out. I buy it at whole foods, and they now carry it in a couple of varieties, including rib eye steak, flank steak, strip steak and ground bison. It's only recently become available in a variety of cuts, but it's a great alternative red meat. The bowl in this picture is the mixture I prepared to roll into the tortilla on the adjoining page. It's a mixture of veggies and cut-up Bison.

YIELD: 4 servings
COOK TIME: 30 minutes

1 cup cooked rice
1 (12 to 16-ounce) bison flank, or strip steak
2 tablespoons grapeseed, canola or peanut oil
½ onion, sliced
½ pepper (red, green and/or yellow)

Cook the rice according to package directions, and set aside.
 Preheat a grill, propane, gas or wood-burning smoker to 350 degrees F.
 Grill the bison for 5 to 7 minutes. It will be rare. Set it aside for 5 minutes. Then cut the meat into 1-inch strips.
 Add the oil to a cast-iron skillet over medium heat, and sauté the onion, peppers, garlic, jalapeño, and mushrooms for 5 minutes until tender. Add the bison strips to the skillet, stir to combine, and cook for 2 minutes until warmed. Do not overcook the bison.
 Wrap the tortillas in foil, and warm them on low-heat (250 degrees F) in the oven for 5 minutes. Then add a portion of the bison mixture to each tortilla center and roll up.
 Serve with warm rice, mashed avocado, or guacamole (recipe, page 23), and pureed black beans on the side.

GROUPER SANDWICH ON BRIOCHE BUN WITH MUSTARD SAUCE

YIELD: 2 sandwiches
COOK TIME: 10 minutes

MUSTARD SAUCE
1 tablespoon Coleman's dry mustard
1 cup mayonnaise
2 teaspoons Worcestershire sauce
1 teaspoon A-1 steak sauce
1 tablespoon light cream
Salt to taste

GROUPER SANDWICH
1 tablespoon grape, peanut or canola oil
12 ounces grouper
2 brioche buns
1 tablespoon mustard sauce
1 Romaine lettuce leaf
1 tomato slice

To make the mustard sauce, combine the dry mustard, mayonnaise, Worcestershire sauce, A-1 steak sauce, and cream. Add salt to taste. Set sauce aside to dress the sandwich.

Heat the oil on a griddle or in cast-iron skillet over medium heat, and sauté both sides of grouper about 5 minutes, turning once, until cooked. Warm the halves of brioche on the same griddle.

Spread the mustard sauce on both sides of roll, and assemble the remainder of sandwich with grouper, lettuce, and tomato, and serve immediately.

Brioche buns are the best—especially when warmed on a griddle. We love this sandwich, as it reminds us of being at the beach in Florida or the Caribbean.

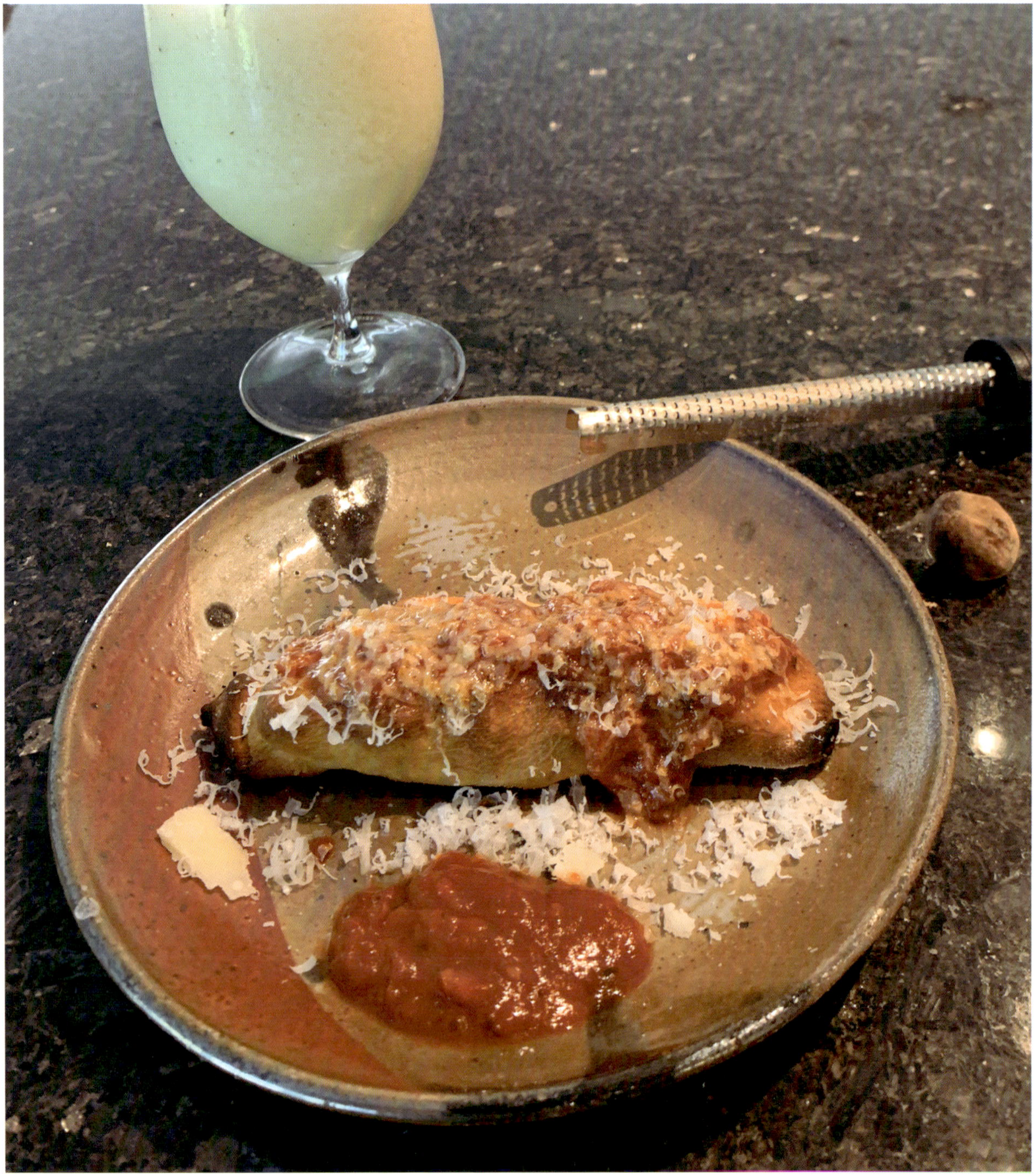

ANDOUILLE & MOZZARELLA CALZONE

YIELD: Serves 1 to 2
COOK TIME: 15 minutes, plus time to make the dough

---

1 pizza shell, fresh or frozen (recipe, page 114)
¼ cup tomato sauce (recipe, page 116)
Oil for the pan
½ andouille sausage

½ cup shaved mozzarella cheese, plus some for garnish
Fresh oregano, for garnish

Make the pizza dough, or buy pre-made dough, fresh or frozen, from a local grocery (I buy ours from Whole Foods, Fresh Market, or Trader Joe's).

Make tomato sauce, or buy premade sauce (I like Rao's).

Preheat an oven to 550 degrees F (or at the highest temperature of your oven).

Roll out the pizza dough to a 10 to 12-inch circle.

Add the oil to a sauté pan over medium heat, and cook the andouille about 5 minutes until cooked through.

Fill the middle of the rolled-out pizza dough with the cooked andouille, half of the tomato sauce, and the mozzarella, and fold over, creating a crescent shape. Pinch the edges to close.

Place it on a pizza stone and bake 10 minutes, or until browned.

Serve hot, sprinkled with some shaved mozzarella, and with a dollop of the remaining tomato sauce on the side.

PIZZA DOUGH

You can use all-purpose flour for this recipe, or better yet, 'zero-zero' (00) flour. 00 is a very finely milled Italian flour which is readily available at local grocery stores. You can also use some whole wheat flour mixed in with the white flour, using 25-50% whole wheat. This will make for a more granular pizza dough, and it's an interesting alternative.

YIELD: 3 (12-inch) or 6 (6 to 7-inch) crusts
COOK TIME: 1 hour 45 minutes

---

2 teaspoons active dry yeast
1 teaspoon sugar
1¼ cups warm water (105 to 115 degrees F)

3⅓ cups 00 flour, or unbleached all-purpose flour
1½ teaspoon kosher salt
4 teaspoons extra-virgin olive oil, divided

Dissolve the yeast and sugar in a measuring cup filled with 1¼ cups warm water; let stand 3 to 5 minutes until foamy.

Insert a dough hook in your mixer and add flour, salt, and 2 teaspoons extra-virgin olive oil.

With the mixer running from low-to-medium speed, add the yeast liquid as fast as flour will absorb. Process about 5 minutes, or until the dough pulls away from the sides of the bowl and forms a ball.

Place the dough ball on clean, hard surface dusted with flour, and knead for 30 seconds. The dough may remain slightly sticky. Coat the dough evenly with 2 teaspoons olive oil and transfer to a large ziplock bag, seal, and place in a warm place to rise for about 45 minutes.

After it rises, place the dough on a lightly floured surface and punch down; then divide it into 3 to 6 portions, and roll it into desired crust sizes, or roll it into balls and refrigerate them if you aren't cooking immediately.

The dough is ready to use, or can be covered in plastic wrap and refrigerated up to 2 days, or frozen for 3 months.

PIZZA AND SALAD

YIELD: 1 (6 or 12-inch diameter) pizza
COOK TIME: 15 minutes

---

1 pizza dough (recipe, page 114)
¼ cup tomato sauce (recipe, page 116), or canned whole peeled tomatoes, crushed
4 ounces ground mozzarella cheese, or a combination of mozzarella, gruyere, Parmesan and provolone

---

Prepare the pizza dough according to the recipe.

Preheat the oven to 550 degrees F, or as hot as your oven heats.

Place a pizza stone in the oven, and preheat for 30 minutes to get the stone very hot.

On a clean, hard surface dusted with flour, roll out 1 ball of dough.

Brush on a light coating of tomato sauce, or spread with whole crushed canned tomatoes.

Cover with mozzarella cheese. For this, I used a combination of cheeses: mozzarella, gruyere, Parmesan and provolone. Choose your favorites. Then top with whatever veggies or meat you like (mushrooms, pepperoni, garlic, olives, peppers, etc.). The pizza shown is topped with thin sliced pepperoni, chopped arugula, and green onions.

Lightly dust the hot pizza stone with corn meal, and place the pizza on it. Return to the oven, and bake for 10 minutes.

Serve with Simple Green Salad with vinaigrette (recipe, page 37).

PEPPERONI PIZZA

YIELD: 1 (6 or 12-inch diameter) pizza
COOK TIME: 20 minutes, plus time to make dough

Pizza dough (recipe, page 114, or use fresh or frozen from a grocery)
2 tablespoons flour
2 tablespoons corn meal, to sprinkle on work surface to keep the dough from sticking
¼ cup tomatoes, chopped/crushed, or tomato sauce
1 tablespoon herbs, such as oregano, chili peppers

2 ounces shredded mozzarella cheese
2 ounces pepperoni, sliced and diced
2 ounces Parmesan cheese, shredded

OPTIONAL
2 tablespoons peppers
2 tablespoons mushrooms
2 tablespoons onions

Preheat the oven to 550 degrees F, or as high as your oven heats.

Let the dough warm to room temperature, then roll out 1 dough ball onto a wooden board or clean, hard surface sprinkled with corn meal. Roll it out as thin as possible.

Top the pizza dough with crushed tomatoes or tomato sauce, herbs, mozzarella cheese, and whatever herbs you prefer. Cook for 10 minutes, or until crispy and browned.

Sprinkle with Parmesan cheese before serving.

PIZZA TOMATO SAUCE

YIELD: 2 cups
COOK TIME: 30 minutes

---

2 tablespoons extra-virgin olive oil
½ onion, chopped
2 cloves garlic, finely chopped

1 (16-ounce) can whole peeled tomatoes
Fresh oregano and/or basil
Pinch of salt and pepper

Add the olive oil to a large sauté pan over medium heat, and sauté the onions and garlic for 5 minutes until they are translucent. Add the tomatoes, and crush with the back of a spoon. Bring the sauce to a simmer, and cook for 30 to 60 minutes, adding the herbs the last 15 minutes.

Add salt and pepper to taste. This sauce will keep, refrigerated, up to 1 week.

Pizza with pepperoni

With 4 cheeses, mushrooms, diced onions and ground meat

Uncooked pizza, ready for oven

Pizza with black and green olives

117

ANGEL HAIR PASTA

Butter and olive oil serve as the sauce base, emulsifying all the other liquid that comes from the sweated vegetables. The addition of the starch-filled pasta water liquifies the sauce and helps bring everything together as it evaporates, allowing it to stick to the pasta.

YIELD: 4 servings
COOK TIME: 15 minutes

1 teaspoon salt (Maldon, or comparable), plus more for seasoning the asparagus	1 clove garlic, diced
16 ounces angel hair pasta	1 onion, diced
2 tablespoons extra-virgin olive oil	1 pepper (red, green and/or yellow), diced
2 tablespoons butter	1 bunch asparagus spears, cut in 1 to 2-inch lengths

Cook the pasta according to package directions until tender but al dente; set aside. Reserve 1 cup of the pasta water to use with the liquid for the sauce.

To make the sauce, heat the oil and butter in a sauté pan over medium heat, and sauté the garlic, onion, and peppers for 5 minutes.

Toss the pasta in the pan of sauce, and stir about 5 minutes, slowly adding 1 cup pasta water a little at a time to thicken (the starch in the water adds a thickener).

Steam the asparagus for 5 minutes in a pot with 2 to 4-inches of boiling water. Then drain, and drizzle with extra-virgin olive oil and salt. Toss into the pasta mixture.

SPINACH PASTA

YIELD: 2 servings
COOK TIME: 15 minutes

2 tablespoons kosher salt	2 tablespoons butter
16 ounces angel hair pasta	1 onion, diced
2 cloves garlic, minced	8 ounces raw spinach, chopped
2 tablespoons extra-virgin olive oil	2 tablespoons fresh parsley, chopped

Cook the pasta according to package directions until tender but al dente; set aside. Reserve 1 cup of the pasta water to use with the liquid for the sauce.

Add the oil and butter to a large sauté pan over medium heat, and sauté the garlic and onions in oil about 5 minutes until translucent. Add the spinach and sauté about 5 minutes until cooked.

Add the cooked pasta and ½ cup of pasta water. Cook at medium-high heat, stirring until a smooth sauce forms. Add a little more water as needed. Garnish with fresh parsley and serve.

PASTA IN RAW TOMATO SAUCE

YIELD: 2 servings
COOK TIME: 30 to 45 minutes

8 ounces angel hair pasta
1 whole tomato, crushed
2 cloves garlic, diced

½ onion, diced
2 tablespoons shredded Parmesan cheese

Cook the pasta according to package directions and set aside, saving ½ cup of the pasta water.
  To make the sauce, crush the whole tomato, and sauté it in a medium pan over medium heat with the garlic and onions to make the sauce. Toss the pasta in the pan with the sauce, top with Parmesan cheese, and serve immediately.

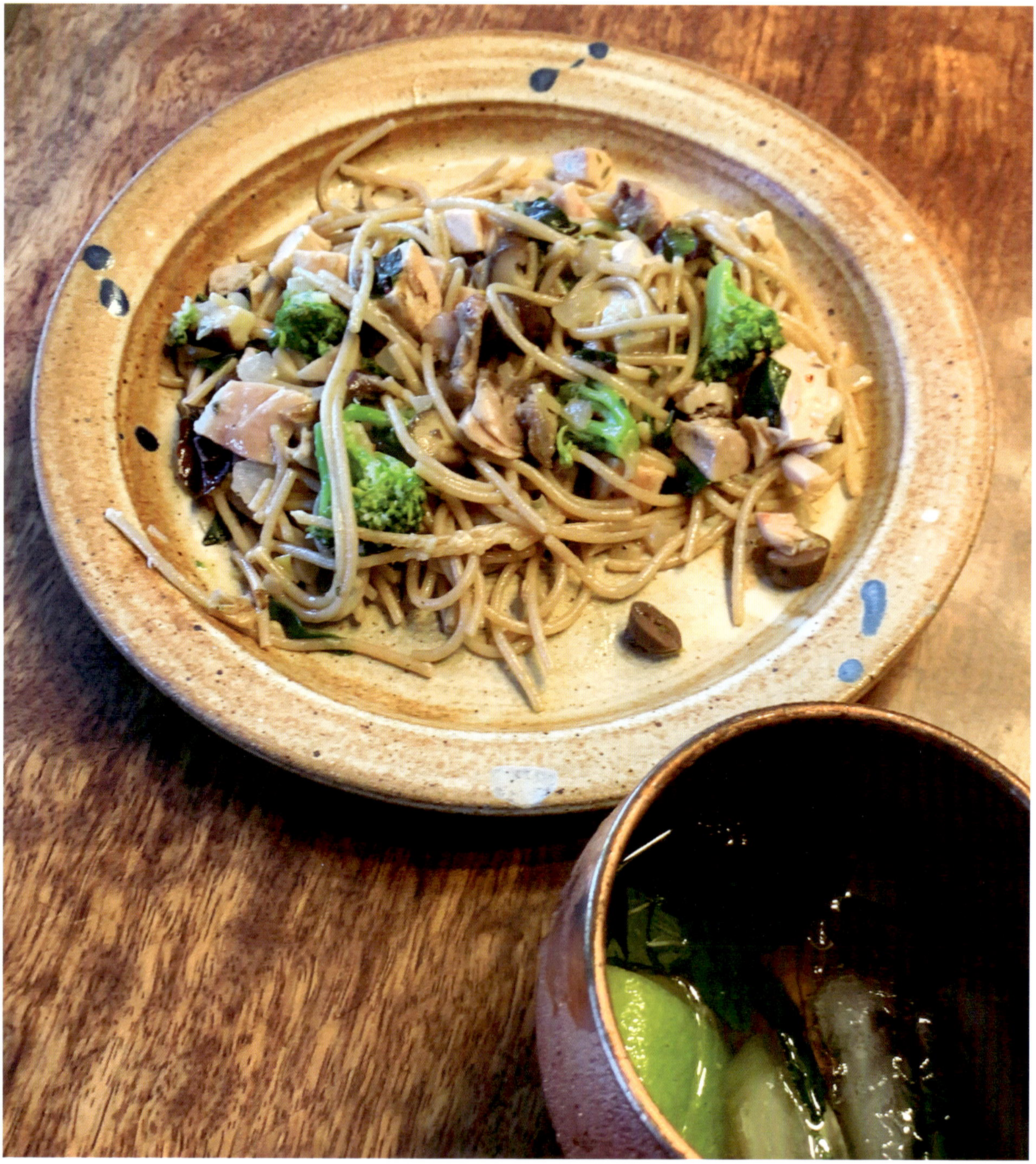

WHOLE WHEAT SPAGHETTI PASTA
WITH CHICKEN AND VEGETABLES

YIELD: 4 servings
COOK TIME: 20 to 30 minutes

16 ounces whole wheat spaghetti pasta
2 tablespoons extra-virgin olive oil
1 head broccoli
1 onion, chopped
2 cloves garlic, minced
2 ounces shiitake mushrooms, sliced
8 ounces rainbow chard, chopped
8 ounces chicken, cubed
2 tablespoons extra-virgin olive oil
2 tablespoons butter
1 tablespoon dried or fresh basil
¼ cup Parmesan, shredded

Cook pasta according to package directions, and set aside.
 Add the oil to a 12-inch skillet over medium heat, and sauté the broccoli, onions, garlic, mushrooms, chicken, and rainbow chard for 5 minutes until tender.
 Add the pasta to the skillet, and stir in the extra-virgin olive oil and butter. Top the pasta mixture with basil, sprinkle with Parmesan, and serve hot.

CHICKEN & ANDOUILLE PAELLA

I learned to make Paella during a trip to Spain while watching it prepared at a party for a large crowd. It's basically an all-in-one pan dish with a rice base. The rice is a particular rice, La Bamba, from Valencia, Spain. In many ways, it's the Spanish national dish. It's great for a party since it's all prepared in one pan, and it can be customized with a variety of proteins, including shellfish, chicken, rabbit and sausage, as well as with vegetables. In addition to being colorful and fun, it tastes great and goes a long way. It's best served with a homemade Sangria, either white or red, which is a combination of dry wine and fruit with a small amount of liquor.

YIELD: 6 to 8 servings
COOK TIME: 45 minutes

---

8 cups chicken (or fish stock if you are including fish as a protein)

1 teaspoon saffron

¼ cup extra-virgin olive oil, plus more to coat the rice

8 ounces deboned chicken, white or dark (I prefer thigh meat), cut in 1 to 1½-inch cubes

8 ounces of andouille sausage, cut into 1-inch pieces

1 pepper, diced

1 onion, diced

2 cloves garlic, minced

2 ripe tomatoes, cubed

8 ounces bomba rice, or arborio rice

2 tablespoons pimentos, or roasted red peppers

¼ cup chopped fresh parsley

4 to 8 lemon wedges

Preheat the oven to 400 degrees F.

In a medium pot, heat the chicken or fish stock and the saffron. Set aside in a bowl or plate and keep warm.

Add the oil to a paella pan over medium-high heat, and cook the chicken and sausage for 5 to 10 minutes, or until it is thoroughly cooked, but rare, and the chicken is browned on all sides. Set aside.

In the same pan over medium heat, sauté the pepper, onion, garlic, tomatoes, and pimentos for 5 minutes. Add chicken and sausage back to veggie mixture; increase the heat to medium-high, and cook for 5 minutes.

Add the uncooked rice to the paella pan over medium heat, and add enough oil to coat the rice thoroughly. Cook for 5 minutes. Stir in the warm chicken stock a few cups at a time to allow it to be absorbed; increase the heat to high, and bring the rice to a boil.

Add the pimentos to the rice mixture. Place the pan in oven and bake uncovered for 15 minutes. Then cover pan with foil, and cook another 15 minutes.

Remove the paella, and let it sit covered on the stove top for 15 minutes.
Sprinkle with fresh parsley, and serve with lemon wedges.

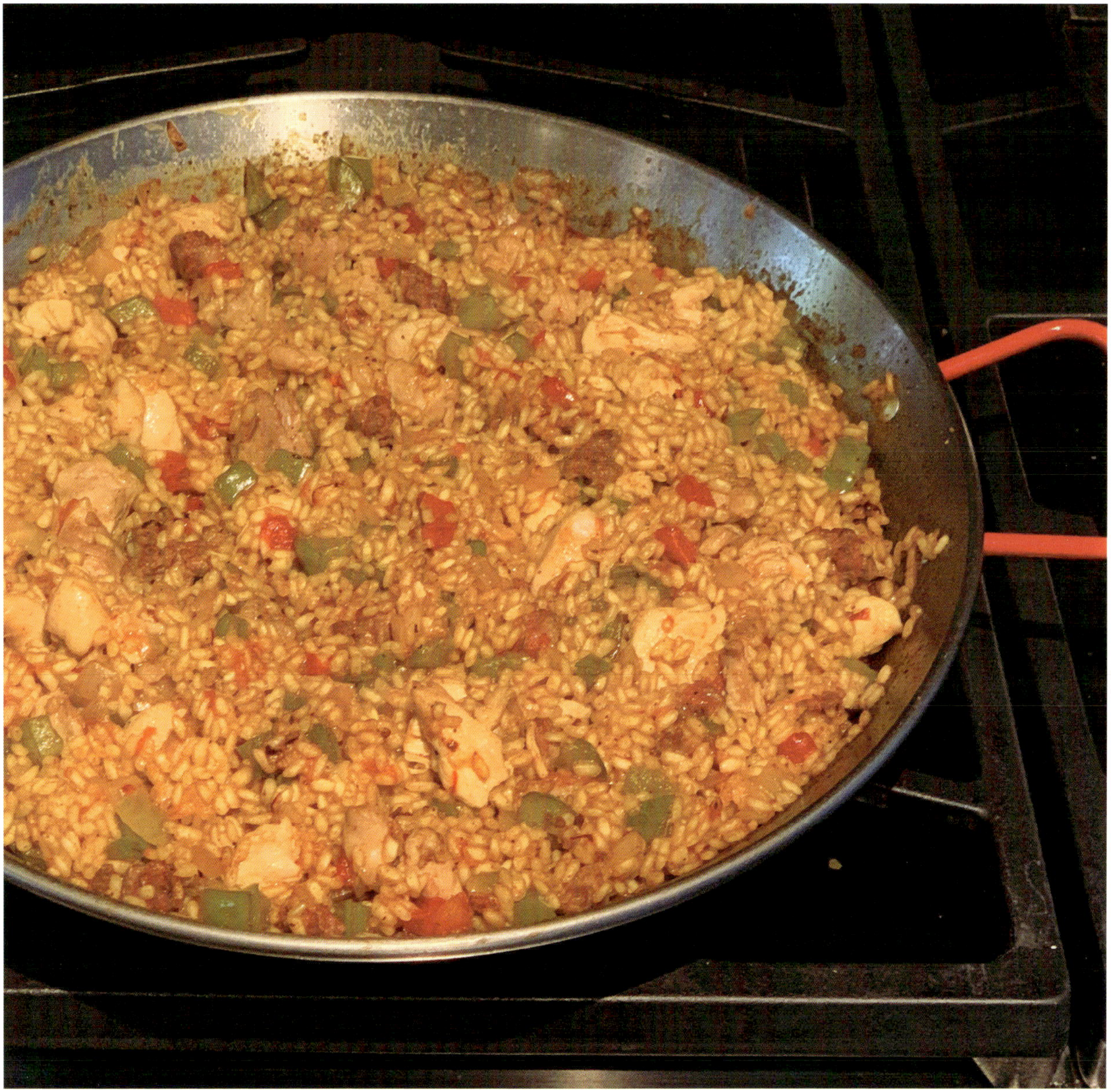

Vegetables & Sides

COLLARD GREENS

VEGETABLE FRIED RICE

BAKED POTATO

STUFFED POTATOES

ROASTED POTATOES

SPINACH

ROASTED CAULIFLOWER

SHAVED ROASTED BRUSSELS SPROUTS

BEETS & GOAT CHEESE

GRILLED EGGPLANT PARMESAN

GRILLED EGGPLANT

STEAMED ARTICHOKES

ROASTED BROCCOLI

WILD MUSHROOM RISOTTO

125

COLLARD GREENS

Since we had so many greens in our garden, it was only natural that we had collard greens on a regular basis. These greens need to be well cooked, since they're not very good undercooked. I prefer using chicken stock; although water or vegetable stock can be used to make it a vegetarian dish. When done, there's always a lot of liquid left in the bottom of the pot—otherwise known as potlikker, a southern tradition—which goes great with bread, muffins, or corn bread.

YIELD: 4 to 8 servings
COOK TIME: 30 to 60 minutes

1 pound collard greens, chopped
2 cups chicken stock, or water
1 onion, chopped
Salt and pepper to taste

Chop the greens, and add to a saucepot along with onion; add salt and pepper to taste.

Fill the pot with 6 inches chicken stock or water. Bring to a simmer over medium-low heat, and cook for 30 to 60 minutes. Continue to add water if the liquid evaporates.

VEGETABLE FRIED RICE

YIELD: 4 servings
COOK TIME: 30 minutes

1 cup cooked brown basmati rice
2 tablespoons canola or peanut oil
1 carrot, diced
½ onion, diced
1 stalk celery, diced
1 clove garlic, minced
2 tablespoons butter
1 egg

Cook the rice according the package directions, and set aside.

Add the oil to a wok, and sauté all vegetables, except the garlic, on high heat for 5 minutes. Once vegetables are soft and translucent, add the garlic and stir for 1 to 2 minutes.

Then add the cooked rice, and toss 5 minutes, or until the rice is hot and begins to get crispy.

Push the rice/vegetable mixture to the edges of the wok, clearing a space in the center and add the butter in the center. Crack the egg over the butter, and scramble with a fork for 1 to 2 minutes.

Stir everything together about 5 minutes so that it's well blended, hot, and crispy.

Serve hot. This dish can keep, covered and refrigerated, for up to 1 week.

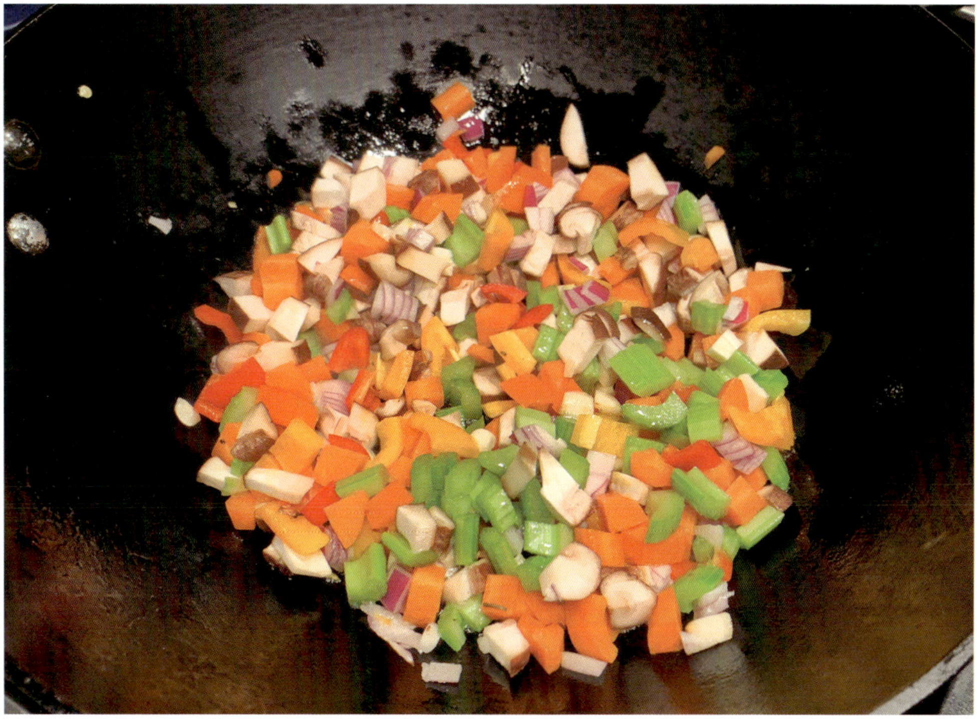

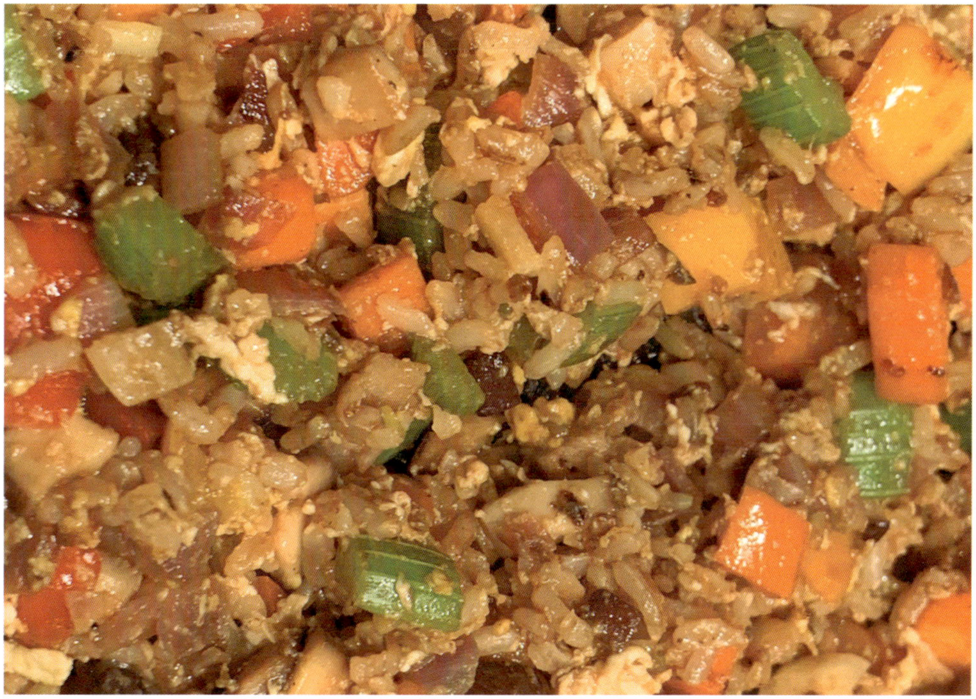

BAKED POTATO

YIELD: 1 serving
COOK TIME: 1 hour

1 potato
High heat oil spray (canola, peanut or grapeseed)
1 tablespoon sour cream
1 tablespoon butter
Salt and pepper to taste

Preheat the oven to 400 degrees F.
 Pierce the potato with a fork, coat with oil, and salt.
 Bake uncovered on the center rack for 1 hour.
 Cut halfway through the potato and stuff with sour cream, butter, and salt and pepper to taste.

STUFFED POTATOES

YIELD: 2 servings
COOK TIME: 15 minutes

8 red bliss potatoes (these are best)
4 ounces blue cheese, cut into 8 small cubes

Preheat the oven to 375 degrees F.
 Boil the potatoes in enough water to cover, and cool enough to handle.
 Core the cooled potatoes with a paring knife, or a melon scooper, to create an area for cheese.
 Stuff each potato with 1 cube blue cheese.
 Bake the stuffed potatoes for 15 minutes 'til they are oozing blue cheese.
 Serve immediately.

ROASTED POTATOES

YIELD: 4 servings
COOK TIME: 45 minutes

1 pound small, round, multi-colored potatoes (white, red or purple, or all of one color)
2 to 4 tablespoons extra-virgin olive oil
Salt to taste

Preheat the oven to 400 degrees F.
 Cut small potatoes in half; toss in a medium bowl with oil and salt to coat potatoes completely.
 Roast them for 45 minutes, or until fork tender and browned.

SAUTEED SPINACH

YIELD: 2 servings
COOK TIME: 15 minutes

2 tablespoons oil
½ onion, diced
2 cloves garlic, minced
16 ounces fresh spinach
Salt and pepper to taste

Add the oil to a saucepan over medium heat, and sauté the onions and garlic for 5 minutes. Add spinach, and stir to coat. Add ½ cup water, and simmer about 15 minutes until tender.
 Add salt and pepper to taste.

ROASTED CAULIFLOWER

YIELD: 2 servings
COOK TIME: 15 minutes

1 whole cauliflower, cut into bite-sized pieces
2 tablespoons extra-virgin olive oil
Salt and pepper to taste

Preheat the oven to 400 degrees F.
Toss the cauliflower pieces with the olive oil, salt, and pepper.
 Place the cauliflower in cast-iron skillet, and roast for 30 minutes until tender and lightly browned.

BRUSSELS SPROUTS

YIELD: 4 servings
COOK TIME: 30 minutes

---

1 pound Brussels sprouts
1/2 cup pecans, chopped and toasted
2 tablespoons extra-virgin olive oil
Salt

Preheat the oven to 375 degrees F.
  In a dry frying pan, toss the pecans over medium heat for 5 to 10 minutes until they start to have a fragrance.
  Shave the sprouts using a Madeline, or cut in small strips with a knife.
  In a medium bowl, toss the sprouts with the extra-virgin olive oil and the pecans, and season with salt to taste.
  Place in a cast-iron skillet and roast for 30 minutes.

ROASTED BEETS AND GOAT CHEESE

YIELD: 4 servings
COOK TIME: 15 minutes

---

2 pounds beets, red and/or yellow

DRESSING
2 tablespoons white wine vinegar
2 tablespoons orange juice
1½ teaspoons grated orange peel
4 tablespoons extra-virgin olive oil
Salt and pepper to taste

SALAD
4 large (2 to 3-inch diameter) beets, unpeeled, scrubbed, all but 1 inch of tops removed
4 ounces chilled goat cheese (such as Montrachet), coarsely crumbled
2 tablespoons chopped dill

Both the dressing and beets can be made the day ahead. Cover separately and refrigerate. When you're ready to cook, bring both to room temperature before continuing.

Preheat the oven to 400 F.
  Wrap the beets in aluminum foil, place on baking sheet, and roast for 1 hour.
  Let the beets cool enough to handle, and then peel and cut into ½-inch wedges.
  To make the dressing: In a small bowl, whisk the vinegar and all the citrus. Then drizzle the oil into the mixture while whisking. Season with salt and pepper to taste.
  To make the salad: Mix the beets and dressing in a large bowl, and sprinkle with the dill.
  Divide among the plates and sprinkle with goat cheese.

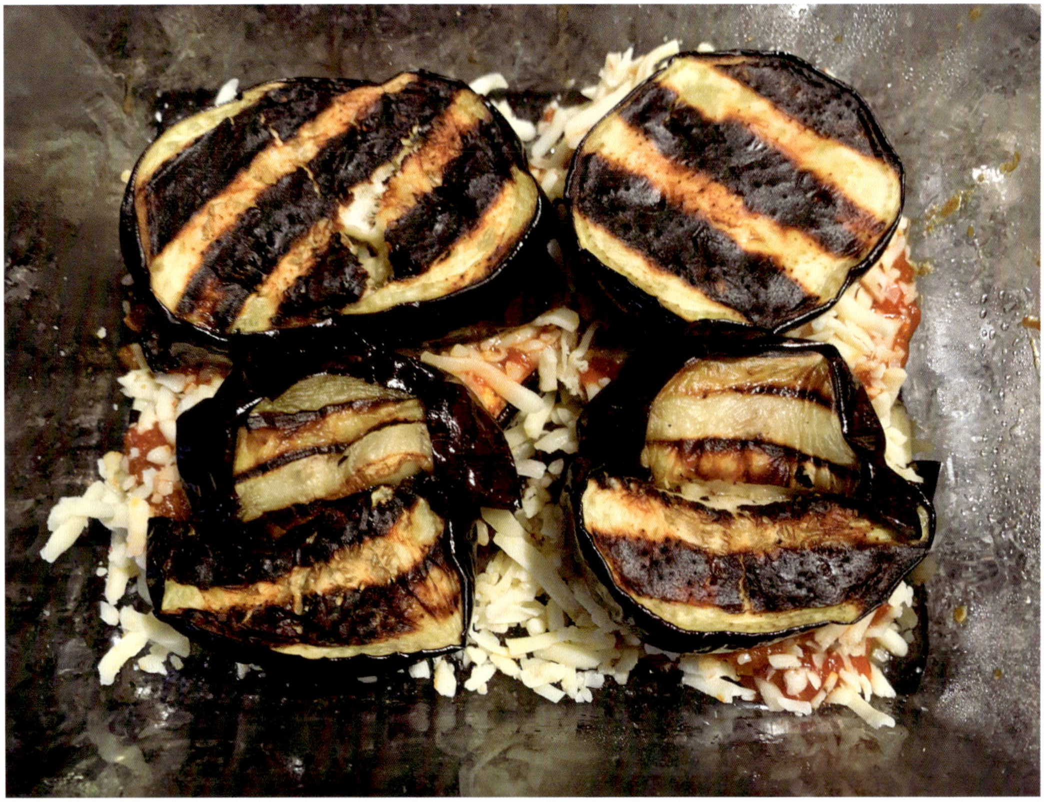

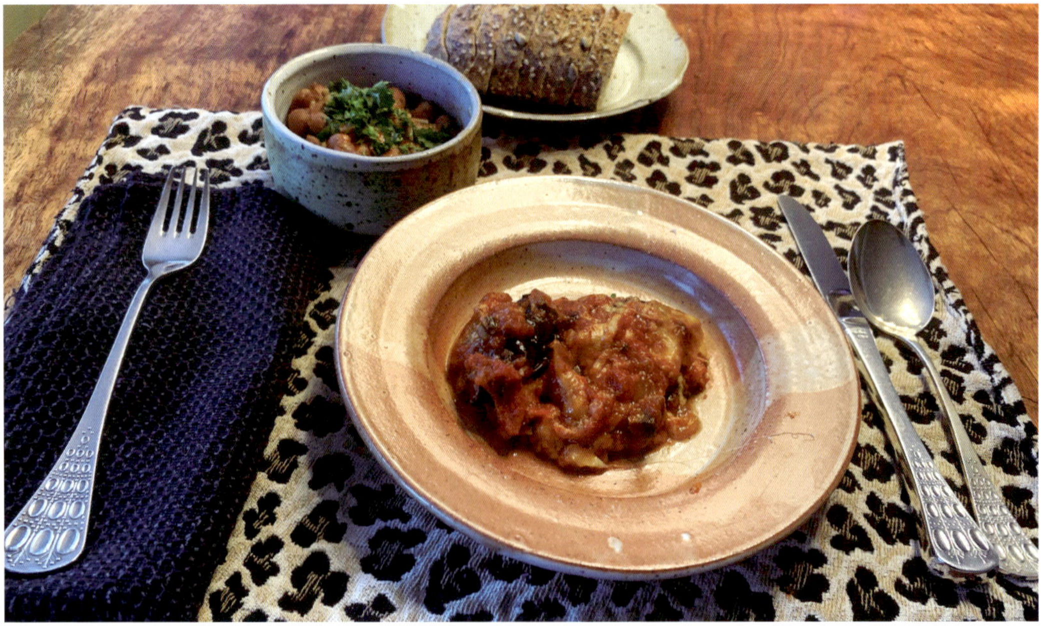

GRILLED EGGPLANT PARMESAN

YIELD: 4 servings, depending on size of eggplant
COOK TIME: 15 to 20 minutes

---

1 eggplant, cut into 2-inch slices, and grilled (recipe below)
4 tablespoons tomato sauce (recipe, page 116, or use Rao's sauce)

4 tablespoons Parmesan cheese, grated
4 tablespoons shredded mozzarella cheese
2 tablespoons chopped fresh parsley

Preheat the oven to 375 degrees F.
 Prepare the grilled eggplant according to the recipe below.
 In a large casserole dish, spread a thin layer of sauce on the bottom of the baking dish, layer the grilled eggplant, top with more tomato sauce, followed by another layer of mozzarella, and sprinkle with Parmesan. This is similar to a grilled eggplant Napoleon. If you'd like, top the top eggplant layer with more tomato and cheese. It's your call.
 Bake for 15 minutes until the top is browned; if the top doesn't brown, you can broil for 2 to 3 minutes until brown.
 Sprinkle each serving with the freshly chopped parsley and serve immediately.

GRILLED EGGPLANT

YIELD: 4 servings, depending on size of eggplant and number of slices
COOK TIME: 45 minutes

---

1 eggplant, cut into 2-inch slices
1 tablespoon salt
Canola, grapeseed, or peanut oil spray

Lay the slices of eggplant on a cookie sheet. Sprinkle salt on both sides, and let them sit 30 minutes.
 Prepare a hot grill.
 After 30 minutes, rinse off the eggplant, and dry with paper towels.
 Spray slices on both sides with canola, grapeseed, or peanut oil.
 Grill the eggplant 5 to 10 minutes, turning every minute or two until soft and nicely marked with grill marks.

STEAMED ARTICHOKES

YIELD: 2 servings
COOK TIME: 1 hour

---

2 tablespoons salt
2 artichokes
Juice of ½ lemon
¼ cup butter, melted

Fill a large pot with 4 inches of water, and add the salt. Bring to boil over high heat.
 Cut the tips off the artichokes with scissors, and remove stem so it can sit flat in bottom of pot. Squeeze the lemon juice onto the artichokes, and place them in the boiling salt water. Add the squeezed lemon halves to the pot.
 Reduce to medium heat; bring the water to a boil, and cook 45 minutes to 1 hour. When you can pull leaves out without much effort, the artichokes are done.
 Serve with melted lemon butter on the side.

ROASTED BROCCOLI

YIELD: 2 to 4 servings
COOK TIME: 30 minutes

---

1 head broccoli, cut into bite-size pieces
1 to 2 tablespoon extra-virgin olive oil
1 teaspoon salt

Preheat the oven to 400 degrees F.
 Toss the broccoli in extra-virgin olive oil and sprinkle with salt.
 Roast in a cast-iron skillet for 20 minutes until fork tender, and serve hot.

WILD MUSHROOM RISOTTO

YIELD: 8 to 9 (1/4 cup) servings
COOK TIME: 30 to 45 minutes

---

2 tablespoons butter
2 tablespoons extra-virgin olive oil
2 small onions, chopped
2 cloves garlic, minced
2 tablespoons chopped fresh thyme
2 tablespoons chopped fresh oregano
2 ounces dried mushrooms re-hydrated (Porcini & Chanterelle, or other exotic mushrooms), or 4 to 6 ounces fresh exotic mushrooms

1 cup white wine
1 pound Arborio rice
9 cups hot chicken broth
1 cup grated Parmesan cheese
½ cup flat leaf parsley
Salt and pepper to taste

10 tablespoons butter (optional, to increase creaminess,

Combine the 2 tablespoons butter, the olive oil, onions, garlic, thyme, and oregano in a large saucepan over medium heat, and cook 5 minutes, or until the onions are translucent.

Rehydrate the mushrooms in 1 cup water, and save the liquid. (If using fresh mushrooms, skip this step.)

Cut the mushrooms into chunks, and add to the onions; cook for 2 minutes. Add the white wine, and cook 2 minutes more, or until the liquid is absorbed.

Stir the rice into the mushroom mixture, along with 1 cup of the rehydrated liquid from the mushrooms, or with 1 cup water, and cook for 8 minutes.

Slowly stir in the hot chicken broth, 1 cup at a time, until the rice becomes creamy.

Cover and cook about 20 minutes, or until the rice is al dente. Then add the Parmesan, parsley, salt, and peppers.

Add the optional butter to increase creaminess, if desired.

Serve warm, as an appetizer, or first course, or as an accompaniment to a main course.

Risotto can be refrigerated and kept for 2 to 3 days, and reheated for future meals.

Drinks

CADILLAC MARGARITA

SIMPLE SYRUP

CUBAN DAQUIRI

FROZEN MARGARITA

YAZI VODKA GINGER MULE

WATERMELON, STRAWBERRY
& PINEAPPLE VODKA SLUSH

TEQUILA DELIGHT

MOSCOW MULE

PIÑA COLADA

CADILLAC MARGARITA

The taste and quality of a great margarita is only as good as the quality of the liquor used.

YIELD: 2 drinks

1 ounce simple syrup (recipe, this page)
Juice of 2 limes
3 ounces premium tequila (Patron Silver)
1 ounce Grand Marnier, or orange liquor
Lime wedges and fresh mint leaves to garnish

Prepare the simple syrup according to recipe, and let it cool.
 Fill a cocktail shaker half full of ice.
 Add all the ingredients to the shaker, and shake to mix until the shaker is frosted.
 Pour 2 (6-ounce) drinks into small cocktail glasses, and fill with ice.
 Garnish with a wedge of lime and fresh mint leaves.

Simple syrup is another kitchen essential for many drinks. In addition, it's fun to have a variety of flavored/herbal simple syrups such as rosemary, basil and/or mint.

SIMPLE SYRUP

YIELD: Enough for 8 drinks
PREP TIME: 5 minutes

8 ounces of sugar or agave syrup
1 cup water

In a small pot over medium heat, stir together 1 cup sugar or agave syrup, and 1 cup water. Heat until the sugar dissolves. Refrigerate until ready to use.

CUBAN DAQUIRI

YIELD: 1 drink

Juice of 1 lime, plus optional zest
1 ounce simple syrup (recipe, page 137)
1½ ounces rum, your choice brand

Put all ingredients in a shaker half filled with ice, and shake until the shaker is frosted. Pour into a small cocktail glass, and top with lime zest (optional).

FROZEN MARGARITA

YIELD: 2 drinks

Salt
Juice of 2 limes
3 ounces premium tequila (Patron Silver)
1 ounce simple syrup (recipe, page 137)
1 ounce Grand Marnier, or orange liquor
1 to 1½ cups crushed ice
Lime wedges and fresh mint leaves, for garnish

Pour a thin layer of salt on a plate. Wet the rim of a drink glass, and roll it in salt.
 In a shaker filled halfway with ice, mix and shake remaining ingredients until the shaker is frosted, about 1 or 2 minutes.
 Pour into a small cocktail glass, and garnish with a wedge of lime and fresh mint leaves.

YAZI VODKA GINGER MULE

YIELD: 1 drink

1½ ounces Yazi ginger flavored vodka
1 ounce lime juice
1 ounce ginger beer
Sprig of mint

Fill a cocktail shaker half way with ice, and add all the ingredients except the mint. Shake until frosty, about 2 minutes.
 Pour into a small cocktail glass with ice, and garnish with mint.

WATERMELON, STRAWBERRY & PINEAPPLE VODKA SLUSH

YIELD: 1 drink

1½ ounce vodka
½ cup each watermelon, strawberry, and pineapple
1 ounce simple syrup (recipe, page 137)
1 cup ice
1 tablespoon finely chopped fresh mint
Splash of ginger beer

Combine all ingredients, except the ginger beer, in a blender; blend until it is "slushy."
 Pour into a small cocktail glass, and top with mint and a splash of Ginger Beer.

Frozen Margarita

Watermelon, Strawberry, & Pineapple Vodka Slush

Yazi Vodka Ginger Mule

Cuban Daquiri

139

TEQUILA DELIGHT

YIELD: 1 serving
PREP TIME: 10 minutes

2 ounces tequila, preferably Patron Silver or similar
Juice of ½ lime
1 ounce simple syrup (recipe, page 137)
Splash of ginger beer
Fresh mint

Combine the tequila, lime juice, and simple syrup in a short cocktail glass full of ice. Top with ginger beer and fresh mint, and serve.

PINA COLADA

YIELD: Serves 1
PREP TIME:

2 ounces coconut cream
1½ ounces rum
3 ounces pineapple juice
Dash of nutmeg
1 cup crushed ice

Mix all the liquids together in a blender with crushed ice for 1 to 2 minutes until it is frozen and slushy. Pour into a tall glass. Top it with a dash of freshly ground nutmeg (or dried will work if you don't have fresh).

MOSCOW MULE

These copper mugs are traditional with moscow mule because they hold the temperature and remain frosty for quite a while.

YIELD: 1 serving
PREP TIME: 15 minutes

2 ounces vodka (premium is best like Chopin or Belvedere)
1 ounce simple syrup (recipe, page 137)
1 ounce ginger beer
Juice of ½ lime, plus a lime wedge
Sprig of fresh mint

Combine vodka, simple syrup, and ginger beer. Serve on ice with mint and lime as garnish. Best served in a metal cup.

INDEX

A

Anchovy fillets: Caesar Salad, 34
Andouille sausage
    Andouille & Chicken Gumbo, 40
    Andouille & Mozzarella Calzone, 113
    Chicken & Andouille Paella, 122
    Fritatta, 99
Angel Hair Pasta, 118
    Chicken Stir Fry, 91
    Grilled Shrimp & Scallops, 69
    Pasta in Raw Tomato Sauce, 63, 119
    Spinach Pasta, 118
    Steamed Mussels in Pasta, 52
Artichokes, Steamed, 134
Arugula
    Chopped Salad, 49
    Salad, 35
Asparagus: Angel hair pasta, 118
Avocado
    Avocado Toast, 23
    Beet & Avocado Salad, 36
    Guacamole, 23
    70s Throwback Health Sandwich, 103

B

Bagel, Cured Salmon &, 105
Baked Potato, 128
Barley, Mushroom &, Soup, 44
Beans: Turkey Chili, 46
Beef. *See also* Ground beef
    Beef Sliders, 28
    Bone-in-Filet, 80
    Grilled T-Bone, 75
    Spinalis Cheesesteak Tortilla, 106
    Spinalis Steak, 87
    Steak Fajitas, 83
Beets
    & Avocado Salad, 36
    Roasted Beets and Goat Cheese, 131
Bell peppers
    Andouille & Chicken Gumbo, 40
    Angel hair pasta, 118
    Chicken Kebab, 88
    Chicken Stir Fry, 91
    Chopped Salad, 49

Grilled Bison Tortilla, 109
Grilled Shrimp & Scallops, 69
Grouper Ceviche, 18
Italian Bean Soup, 41
Lobster & Snapper Ceviche, 20
Sautéed Grouper, 60
Shrimp Fajita, 68
Snapper Ceviche, 19
Spinalis Cheesesteak Tortilla, 106
Steak Fajitas, 83
Steamed Mussels in Pasta, 52
Bison
    Grilled Bison Tortilla, 109
    Lasagna, 85
Black beans: Shrimp Fajita, 68
Blue cheese
    Chopped Salad, 49
    Stuffed Potatoes, 128
Bone-in-Fillet, 80
Botham Burgers, 102
Broccoli
    Roasted, 134
    Thai Chili Shrimp, 67
    Whole Wheat Spaghetti Pasta, 121
Brown rice. *See also* Rice
    Sautéed Grouper, 60
    Shrimp Fajita, 68
    Thai Chili Shrimp, 67
    Vegetable Fried Rice, 126
Brussels Sprouts, 130
Bulgur wheat: Tabouleh, 22

C

Cadillac Margarita, 137
Caesar Salad, 34
Calzone, Andouille & Mozzarella, 113
Cauliflower
    & Ginger Soup, 45
    Roasted, 129
    Thai Chili Shrimp, 67
Ceviche
    Grouper, 18
    Lobster & Snapper, 20
    Snapper, 19
Chard: Whole Wheat Spaghetti Pasta, 121
Cheddar cheese

Botham Burgers, 102
    Mini Grilled Cheese Sandwich, 105
    70s Throwback Health Sandwich, 103
    Turkey Chili, 46
Cheese. *See* Blue cheese; Cheddar cheese; Feta cheese; Gruyere cheese; Mozzarella cheese; Parmesan cheese
Chicken
    Andouille & Chicken Gumbo, 40
    Chicken & Andouille Paella, 122
    Chicken Kebab, 88
    Chicken Noodle Soup, 38
    Chicken Pad Thai, 92
    Chicken & Shrimp Kebab, 89
    Chicken Stir Fry, 91
    Chicken Stock, 38
    Italian Bean Soup, 41
    Spatchcocked Chicken, 86
    Whole Wheat Spaghetti Pasta, 121
Chickpeas: Hummus/Tahini, 21
Chili, Turkey, 46
Chopped Salad, 49
Collard Greens, 126
Colossal Shrimp, 24
Corn: Crawfish Boil, 56
Cornish Hen, 95
Crab Cakes, 55
Crawfish Boil, 56
Cuban Daquiri, 138
Cucumber, Tomato & Feta Salad, 36
Cured Salmon, 31
Cured Salmon & Bagel, 105

E

Eggplant
    Grilled, 133
    Grilled, Parmesan, 133
Eggs
    Avocado Toast, 23
    Fritatta, 99
    Hole-in-One, 100

F

Feta cheese, Cucumber, Tomato, Salad, 36
Fish & seafood

INDEX

Caesar Salad, 34
Chicken & Shrimp Kebab, 89
Colossal Shrimp, 24
Crab Cakes, 55
Crawfish Boil, 56
Cured Salmon, 31
Grilled Salmon, 64
Grilled Shrimp & Scallops, 69
Grilled Shrimp Soup, 42
Grilled Striped Bass, 71
Grouper Ceviche, 18
Grouper Sandwich on Brioche Bun
   with Mustard Sauce, 110
Lobster & Snapper Ceviche, 20
Mahi-Mahi Fillets, 63
Sautéed Grouper, 60
Shrimp Fajita, 68
Snapper Ceviche, 19
Steamed Mussels in Pasta, 52
Stone Crab Claws, 59
Thai Chili Shrimp, 67
Focaccia, 26
Fritatta, 99
Frozen Margarita, 138

G

Garlic Aioli, 55
Ginger, Cauliflower &, Soup, 45
Goat cheese, Roasted Beets and, 131
Greens. *See also* Lettuce; Romaine lettuce
  Chicken & Shrimp Kebabs, 89
  Italian Bean Soup, 41
Grilled Caesar Salad, 35
Grilled Cheesecake Tortilla, 106
Grilled Eggplant, 133
Grilled Eggplant Parmesan, 133
Grilled Lamb Chops, 79
Grilled Salmon, 64
Grilled Shrimp & Scallops, 69
Grilled Shrimp Soup, 42
Grilled Striped Bass, 71
Grilled T-Bone, 75
Ground beef
  Beef Sliders, 28
  Botham Burgers, 102

Grouper
  Ceviche, 18
  Grouper Sandwich on Brioche Bun, 110
  Sautéed Grouper, 60
Gruyere cheese: Fritatta, 99
Guacamole, 23
  Shrimp Fajita, 68

H

Hole-in-One, 100
Hummus/Tahini, 21

I

Italian Bean Soup, 41

J

Jalapeño pepper
  Chicken Pad Thai, 92
  Grouper Ceviche, 18
  Lobster & Snapper Ceviche, 20
  Snapper Ceviche, 19

K

Kebabs
  Chicken Kebab, 88
  Chicken & Shrimp Kebab, 89
Kidney beans: Turkey Chili, 46

L

Lamb
  Grilled Lamb Chops, 79
  Rack of Lamb, 76
  Roasted Leg of Lamb, 78
Lasagna, Bison, 85
Leeks: Fritatta, 99
Lettuce. *See also* Greens; Romaine lettuce
  Botham Burgers, 102
  Cured Salmon & Bagel, 105
  70s Throwback Health Sandwich, 103
  Simple Green Salad, 37
Lobster & Snapper Ceviche, 20

M

Mahi-Mahi Fillets, 63
Mini Grilled Cheese Sandwich, 105
Moscow Mule, 140
Mozzarella cheese
  Andouille & Mozzarella Calzone, 113
  Bison Lasagna, 85
  Grilled Eggplant Parmesan, 133
  Pepperoni Pizza, 116
  Pizza and Salad, 115
  Spinalis Cheesesteak Tortilla, 106
Mushrooms
  Chicken Kebab, 88
  Chicken Pad Thai, 92
  Chicken Stir Fry, 91
  Chopped Salad, 49
  Italian Bean Soup, 41
  Mushroom & Barley Soup, 44
  Shrimp Fajita, 68
  Spinalis Cheesesteak Tortilla, 106
  Whole Wheat Spaghetti Pasta, 121
  Wild Mushroom Risotto, 135
Mussels, Steamed, in Pasta, 52
Mustard Sauce, 59, 110

N

Noodles
  Chicken Noodle Soup, 38
  Chicken Pad Thai, 92

O

Onions
  Angel hair pasta, 118
  Chicken Kebab, 88
  Chicken & Shrimp Kebabs, 89
  Grilled Bison Tortilla, 109
  Shrimp Fajitas, 68
  Spinalis Cheesesteak Tortilla, 106
  Steak Fajitas, 83

P

Parmesan cheese
  Arugula Salad, 35

Bison Lasagna, 85
Caesar Salad, 34
Grilled Eggplant Parmesan, 133
Grilled Shrimp & Scallops, 69
Pasta in Raw Tomato Sauce, 63, 119
Pepperoni Pizza, 116
Whole Wheat Spaghetti Pasta, 121
Wild Mushroom Risotto, 135
Pasta in Raw Tomato Sauce, 63, 119
Pepperoni Pizza, 116
Pina Colada, 140
Pineapple: Chicken Kebab, 88
Pita Bread, 26
Pizza and Salad, 115
Pizza Dough, 114
    Pepperoni Pizza, 116
    Pizza and Salad, 115
Pizza Tomato Sauce, 116
Potatoes
    Baked, 128
    Crawfish Boil, 56
    Roasted Potatoes, 129
    Stuffed Potatoes, 128

Q

Quail, Roasted, 95

R

Rack of Lamb, 76
Rice. *See also* Brown rice
    Andouille & Chicken Gumbo, 40
    Chicken & Andouille Paella, 122
    Grilled Bison Tortilla, 109
    Vegetable Fried, 126
    Wild Mushroom Risotto, 135
Roasted Beets and Goat Cheese, 131
Roasted Broccoli, 134
Roasted Cauliflower, 129
Roasted Leg of Lamb, 78
Roasted Potatoes, 129
Roasted Quail, 95
Romaine lettuce
    Caesar Salad, 34
    Chopped Salad, 49
    Grilled Caesar Salad, 35

Grouper Sandwich on Brioche Bun, 110
Shrimp Fajita, 68

S

Salmon. *See under* Fish & seafood
Sautéed Grouper, 60
Sauteed Spinach, 129
Scallops, Grilled Shrimp &, 69
70s Throwback Health Sandwich, 103
Shrimp. *See* Fish & seafood
Simple Green Salad, 37
Simple Syrup, 137
Snapper Ceviche, 19
Spaghetti, Whole Wheat, Pasta, 121
Spatchcocked Chicken, 86
Spinach
    Pasta, 118
    Sauteed, 129
    White Bean &, Soup, 48
Spinalis Cheesesteak Tortilla, 106
Spinalis Steak, 87
Steak Fajitas, 83
Steamed Artichokes, 134
Steamed Mussels in Pasta, 52
Stone Crab Claws, 59
Striped bass, grilled, 71
Stuffed Potatoes, 128

T

Tabouleh, 22
Tequila Delight, 140
Thai Chili Shrimp, 67
Tomatoes
    Beet & Avocado Salad, 36
    Bison Lasagna, 85
    Botham Burgers, 102
    Chicken & Andouille Paella, 122
    Cucumber, Tomato & Feta Salad, 36
    Cured Salmon & Bagel, 105
    Grouper Sandwich on Brioche Bun, 110
    Guacamole, 23

Lobster & Snapper Ceviche, 20
Pasta in Raw Tomato Sauce, 63, 119
Pepperoni Pizza, 116
Pizza and Salad, 115
70s Throwback Health Sandwich, 103
Snapper Ceviche, 19
Tabouleh, 22
Turkey Chili, 46
Tortillas
    Grilled Bison Tortilla, 109
    Spinalis Cheesesteak Tortilla, 106
Turkey bacon, Hole-in-One, 100
Turkey Chili, 46

V

Vegetable Fried Rice, 126

W

Watermelon Strawberry & Pineapple Vodka Slush, 138
White Bean & Spinach Soup, 48
Whole Wheat Spaghetti Pasta, 121
Wild Mushroom Risotto, 135

Y

Yazi Vodka Ginger Mule, 138

ACKNOWLEDGEMENTS

I'd like to acknowledge the Critic, Robin Pollack, for putting up with my food experimentation all these years. She's always so kind about her criticism.

In addition, I need to acknowledge all of those who helped me with this book, including Janice Shay, the book whisperer, Carol Book, Sa & Kaa, Annette Joseph—stylist *extraordinaire*, fabulous photographer Deborah Whitlaw Llewellyn, Giovanni DePalma who makes the best pizzas on earth, Zeb Stephenson—one of the most aspiring young chefs in the ATL, and Jenny Levenson, aka "Souper Jenny," the Buckhead Rockstar, always comforting the community with her multifaceted, do-good attitude and warm, comforting environment and food.

I'd be remiss if I didn't acknowledge all our friends who have put up with dinner at Chez Marc, including Ricky & Lois, Sharon & Roger, Clive/Saa & Barry/Ka, and Adam & Beth.

Finally, thank you to all the great chefs and foodies in ATL and around the world who have inspired me and taught me everything I know.

The author spent forty years investing in multifamily real estate around the southeastern US. After an exciting, highly successful career culminating in the organization of Pollack Shores Real Estate Group (now known as RangeWater Real Estate), Marc decided to return to his roots in the social service and non-profit sector. Marc is an active participant on numerous boards and other endeavors in the areas of affordable housing and homelessness. Through it all, Marc's single hobby has always been cooking—that is, food and wine. So, The Quarantine Cookbook *is a dream come true; an opportunity to come full circle and to share his passion with a broader audience.*

Copyright 2020 by Marc S. Pollack
All rights reserved

Printed in Canada

Design by Janice Shay / Pinafore Press
Photography by Marc S. Pollack
Cover photography, and on pages *4 and 10*, by Deborah Whitlaw Llewellyn, DWL Photography
Index by Sandi Shroeder Indexing Servicees

ISBN 978-0-578-78944-6

MARRO Publishing, Atlanta GA